MW00647561

The Thin Red Line

The Thin Red Line is the third feature-length film from acclaimed director Terrence Malick, set during the struggle between American and Japanese forces for Guadalcanal in the South Pacific during World War Two. It is a powerful, enigmatic, and complex film that raises important philosophical questions, ranging from the existential and phenomenological to the artistic and technical.

This is one of the first collections dedicated to exploring the philosophical aspects of Malick's film. Opening with a helpful introduction that places the film in context, five essays, four of which were specially commissioned for this collection, go on to examine the following:

- the exploration of Heideggerian themes—such as being-towards-death and the vulnerability of Dasein's world—in *The Thin Red Line*
- how Malick's film explores and cinematically expresses the embodied nature of our experience of, and agency in, the world
- Malick's use of cinematic techniques, and how the style of his images shapes our affective, emotional, and cognitive responses to the film
- the role that images of nature play in Malick's cinema, and his "Nietzschean" conception of human nature.

The Thin Red Line is essential reading for students interested in philosophy and film or phenomenology and existentialism. It also provides an accessible and informative insight into philosophy for those in related disciplines such as film studies, literature, and religion.

Contributors: Simon Critchley, Hubert Dreyfus and Camilo Prince, David Davies, Amy Coplan, Iain Macdonald.

David Davies is Associate Professor of Philosophy at McGill University. He is the author of *Art as Performance* (2004) and *Aesthetics and Literature* (2007).

Philosophers on Film

The true significance of film for philosophy, and of philosophy for film, cannot be established in abstract or general terms. It can only be measured in and through individual philosophers' attempts to account for their experience of specific films. This series promises to provide a productive context for that indispensable enterprise.

Stephen Mulhall, Fellow and Reader in
Philosophy, New College, Oxford

Film is increasingly used to introduce and discuss key topics and problems in philosophy, whilst some films raise important philosophical questions of their own. Yet until now, dependable resources for those studying and teaching philosophy and film have been limited. *Philosophers on Film* answers this growing need and is the first series of its kind.

Each volume assembles a team of international contributors who explore a single film in depth. Beginning with an introduction by the editor, each specially-commissioned chapter discusses a key aspect of the film in question. Additional features include a biography of the director and suggestions for further reading, making the series ideal for anyone studying philosophy, film and anyone with a general interest in the philosophical dimensions of cinema.

Forthcoming:

* *Eternal Sunshine of the Spotless Mind*, edited by Christopher Grau
* *Memento*, edited by Andrew Kania
* *Blade Runner*, edited by Amy Coplan
* *Talk to Her*, edited by A.W. Eaton

The Thin Red Line

Edited by

David Davies

Routledge
Taylor & Francis Group
LONDON AND NEW YORK

This edition published 2009
by Routledge
2 Park Square, Milton Park, Abingdon, Oxon, OX14 4RN

Simultaneously published in the USA and Canada
by Routledge
711 Third Avenue, New York, NY 10017

Routledge is an imprint of the Taylor & Francis Group, an informa business

© 2009 David Davies for selection and editorial matter; individual
contributors for their contributions

Typeset in Joanna by
Florence Production Ltd, Stoodleigh, Devon

All rights reserved. No part of this book may be reprinted or
reproduced or utilized in any form or by any electronic, mechanical,
or other means, now known or hereafter invented, including photocopying
and recording, or in any information storage or retrieval system,
without permission in writing from the publishers.

British Library Cataloguing in Publication Data
A catalogue record for this book is available from the British Library

Library of Congress Cataloguing in Publication Data
The Thin Red Line/edited by David Davies.
        p. cm.—(Philosophers on film)
    Includes bibliographical references and index.
    1. Thin red line (Motion picture).   I. Davies, David.
    PN1997.T28533T35 2008
    791.43'72—dc22   2008011219

ISBN10: 0–415–77364–4 (hbk)
ISBN10: 0–415–77365–2 (pbk)

ISBN13: 978–0–415–77364–5 (hbk)
ISBN13: 978–0–415–77365–2 (pbk)

Contents

Illustrations

Contributor biographies

Amy Coplan is Assistant Professor of Philosophy at California State University, Fullerton. Her primary areas of research are philosophy of emotion, ancient Greek philosophy, and philosophy of film. She has published on questions regarding empathy, emotional contagion, and emotional engagement with film. She is currently co-editing an interdisciplinary collection on empathy and editing a book on Ridley Scott's *Blade Runner* for this series.

Simon Critchley is Professor of Philosophy at the New School for Social Research, New York. He is author of many books, including *On Humour* (Routledge, 2002), *Things Merely Are* (Routledge, 2005), and most recently *Infinitely Demanding* (Verso, 2007). His *The Book of Dead Philosophers* is published in 2008 by Granta in the United Kingdom and by Vintage in the USA.

David Davies is Associate Professor in the Department of Philosophy at McGill University. He is the author of *Art as Performance* (Blackwell, 2004) and *Aesthetics and Literature* (Continuum, 2007), and has published on issues in the philosophies of film, photography, literature, and the visual arts, and on topics in metaphysics, philosophy of mind, philosophy of language, and philosophy of science.

Hubert Dreyfus is Professor of Philosophy in the Graduate School at the University of California at Berkeley. His publications include: *What Computers (Still) Can't Do* (Cambridge, MA: MIT Press, 1992); *Being-in-the-World: A Commentary on Division I of Heidegger's* Being and Time (Cambridge, MA: MIT Press, 1991); (with Stuart Dreyfus) *Mind Over Machine; The Power of Human Intuition and Expertise in the Era of the Computer* (Free Press, 1986), and, most recently, *On the Internet* (Routledge, 2001).

Iain Macdonald is *professeur agrégé* in the Department of Philosophy at the Université de Montréal and adjunct Professor in the Department of Philosophy at McGill University. He has published in English and French on Hegel, Adorno, and Heidegger. His research focuses on the intersection of epistemology, metaphysics, and normativity.

Camilo Salazar Prince studied philosophy at UC Berkeley. He is now finishing his debut film, *Cienfuegos*.

Note on the director

Terrence Malick was born in November 1943 in Ottawa, Illinois (or possibly in Waco, Texas), and grew up in Oklahoma and Texas. He studied philosophy at Harvard, working with Stanley Cavell, before going to Magdalen College, Oxford, on a Rhodes Scholarship. His intention was to work, under the supervision of Gilbert Ryle, on a thesis on the concept of world in Kierkegaard, Heidegger, and Wittgenstein, but, unsurprisingly perhaps, Ryle was not greatly enamoured with the project. Malick returned to the United States without completing his thesis, and seemed destined for a career in academic philosophy. He taught phenomenology at MIT as a leave replacement for Hubert Dreyfus, and published, in 1969, his translation of Heidegger's *Vom Wesen des Grundes* as *The Essence of Reasons* (Evanston, IL: Northwestern University Press).

In the same year, however, he enrolled in the inaugural class at the Center for Advanced Film Studies at the American Film Institute in Los Angeles. There, in 1969, he produced the eighteen-minute film *Lanton Miles*, which was shown at an early screening of *Badlands*, but subsequently withdrawn. For a couple of years, he worked in Hollywood as screen-writer and script doctor on a number of undistinguished films (see Morrison and Schur 2003: 2–8 for details of Malick's activities at this time). He received independent financial support to make *Badlands*, a film loosely based on a series of apparently random killings carried out by Charlie Starkweather in the American midwest in 1958. Drawing considerable praise when screened at the New York Film Festival in autumn 1973, the film was bought and distributed by Warner Brothers. Malick's second film, *Days of Heaven*, set in the Texas panhandle during World War I, went into production in 1976 with a much more substantial budget from Paramount, but was not released until 1978 after considerable editing in post-production.

After the release of *Days of Heaven*, Malick appears to have left Hollywood, possibly moving to France. He returned to cinema in 1998 with *The Thin Red Line*, based on James Earl Jones' novel chronicling the American battle for Guadalcanal in World War II. The film again underwent considerable changes during post-production. When released, it polarized reviewers—it was nominated for seven Academy Awards but did not receive any—and there is wide critical disagreement as to its thematic content. Malick's most recent film, *The New World* (2005), is a re-telling of the story of John Smith and Pocahontas, which bears some close resemblances, stylistically and thematically, to *The Thin Red Line*.

Reference

Morrison, J. and Schur, T. (2003) *The Films of Terrence Malick*, London: Praeger.

Chapter 1

Introduction

I

TERRENCE MALICK IS AMONG THE MOST celebrated and critically acclaimed contemporary American directors. Yet he is also a deeply enigmatic figure whose artistic career is punctuated by a twenty-year absence during which time his whereabouts and activities remain unclear. Malick studiously avoids interactions with the media, giving no interviews since his first film, *Badlands*, in 1973. He has, in over thirty years, directed only four feature films, the others being *Days of Heaven* (1978), *The Thin Red Line* (1998), and *The New World* (2005). His work has, from the first, been described as "poetic" and "visionary," qualities that relate to his often breathtaking use of natural imagery and to his cinematic explorations of human nature and our relationships with the natural world.

It is surprising, given Malick's elevated standing in the pantheon of modern directors, that there are to date few critical studies of his work. Two critical monographs have appeared thus far (Morrison and Schur 2003; Chion 2004), the latter restricting itself to *The Thin Red Line*. Another general monograph is forthcoming (Martin 2008). There is, in addition, an extended treatment of *The Thin Red Line* in a chapter of a book (Bersani and Dutoit 2004), and a comparative assessment with other directors such as David Lynch and Robert Altman in a chapter of a book on contemporary cinema (Orr 1998: 162–87). Prior to the present volume, only one collection of critical articles on Malick's cinema has been published (Patterson, ed., 2003; expanded edition 2007).

Given Malick's philosophical training (see "Note on the director") and the overtly philosophical material in The Thin Red Line, it is not surprising that many commentators, including contributors to the present volume, have sought to locate the film in philosophical space. Later in this Introduction, I shall briefly survey the divergent conceptions of that location and, relatedly, of the role of images of nature in his films. I shall also outline the contributions that the five papers contained in this volume make to furthering our understanding and appreciation of The Thin Red Line. First, however, I shall look at another approach to the film, which sees it as intentionally engaging with generic expectations about "war" movies in order to call into question the adequacy of those expectations to their subject.

II

It is not difficult to assign Malick's films to well-established cinematic genres, and to compare them with other contemporary films belonging to the same genres. Badlands and Penn's Bonnie and Clyde are readily ascribed to the "outlaw/road movie" genre (Campbell 2003; Orr 2003), and much was made, on their release, of the relative virtues of The Thin Red Line and Spielberg's Saving Private Ryan as war movies (see Flanagan 2003). Days of Heaven seems to fall into the genre of Western, and The New World into that of grand historical drama with humanistic intent. But, while all of Malick's films clearly draw upon certain generic expectations in the receiver, commentators have claimed that, given how the films elicit and then fail to satisfy these expectations, this must be done in pursuit of some end other than expanding or renovating the genre.

In the case of The Thin Red Line, taken to be a "war movie" (the DVD of The Thin Red Line appears in the series Fox War Classics), our generic expectations are that the narrative will be tightly structured and will present various scenes of combat action whose purpose is the attainment of some shared goal that is realized, or that tragically fails to be realized, at the end of the film. We expect that the characters will be sharply individuated from one another in order to personalize them for the audience, and that what is achieved will depend upon the different skills and the camaraderie of the "band of brothers" working together. In the case of The Thin Red Line, however, such expectations are constantly frustrated: "many of the characters are indistinguishable from one another. Then there is the great battle, which seems to resolve nothing and serves as an anti-climax" (McGettigan 2003: 50). The generic failings of The Thin Red Line have been seen by some commentators as deliberate devices that serve an ulterior interest in critically undermining the genre and providing a more realistic cinematic representation of the realities of modern warfare (Flanagan 2003). But this reading of the film, like other readings that take its subject to be war in the literal sense, are difficult to square with the role that the film accords to images of nature, and with the overtly philosophical or religious dimension to the voiceovers that punctuate the narrative. Rather than being concerned with subverting generic expectations in the interests of more realistically portraying the realities that are subject to generic representation, one suspects that Malick begins with an alternative conception of his project, one that involves taking, as nominal subject matter, something that would standardly fall within a given cinematic genre, but with other goals in mind. While the "war at the heart of nature" announced as a principal theme of The Thin Red Line in the opening voiceover may be symbolized by the scenes of war in the film, the departures from generic expectations for presenting such scenes can be seen as dictated by the broader interests of this principal theme rather than by an interest in generic subversion.

Most serious interpreters of The Thin Red Line, perhaps aware of these difficulties, have looked elsewhere for the film's intended thematic significance. (For a more extensive review of different interpretations of the film, see Davies, this volume.) A number of critics have seen the narrative as operating at the level of myth rather than history, as an expression of an "Edenic yearning" for a lost wholeness of being, or as an expression of an Emersonian Transcendentalism. The idea here is that Nature and Soul are the elements making up the universe, and that the individual can attain a kind of unity with the world soul through communing with nature. Others, however, aware of Malick's philosophical training, find very different intellectual affinities in the film. They locate it in a more Heideggerian context, as a meditation on mortality and Dasein's being-towards-death, or as a cinematic expression of the Heideggerian ontological critique of technology, and of the Heideggerian role of poet in destitute times who reveals through the medium of cinema the presencing of Being through language.

Associated with these readings of the thematic meaning of The Thin Red Line we find radically opposed interpretations of the many representations of nature in the film. Some see Malick's cinema as expressing a broadly naturalistic conception of nature. Nature, non-enchanted, is a warring force that frames the human drama of war but is utterly indifferent to human purposes and intentions. For others, Malick represents nature as "a powerful sign of a higher good" or as the spiritual realm, communion with which allows us to transcend the individual strivings expressed in war.

III

The chapters in the present volume critically engage with, but go beyond, these more general currents of thought about The Thin Red Line. In so doing, they provide three kinds of philosophical perspectives on Malick's richly textured film. First, they show how a complex cinematic work such as The Thin Red Line can, in more than a merely hyperbolic sense, be regarded as a medium for philosophical reflection. Second, they explore the cinematic techniques through which the philosophical themes in the film are articulated. And third, they enliven debates in the philosophy of film about the ways in which cinematic meaning emerges out of the putting together of image and sound, the role of the emotions in film experience, and the cognitive and moral values rightly ascribable to film as an art. Hubert Dreyfus and Camilo Prince, and Simon Critchley, examine in different ways the manner in which our understanding of broadly Heideggerian themes is explored and deepened in Malick's film, while carefully resisting the "reductive" temptation to see the film as a mere exemplification of such themes. (Critchley writes: "it seems to me that a consideration of Malick's art demands that we take seriously the idea that film is less an illustration of philosophical ideas and theories . . . and more a form of philosophizing, of reflection, reasoning and argument.") Iain Macdonald examines one of the central puzzles in Malick's cinema: the role that is accorded to images of nature. He reads The Thin Red Line through Malick's subsequent work, The New World, which bears an eerie structural and visual resemblance to its predecessor. David Davies examines the thematization in the film of our embodied cognitive engagement with the world, both as perceivers and as agents, and the complex ways in which Malick achieves such a thematization through the manipulation of the different contentful elements that enter into our experience of the film. And Amy Coplan, drawing on a broad understanding of the cinematographic and editorial techniques that enter into the sculpting of the images presented to the receivers of films, explores in greater depth Malick's cinematic style and the ways in which it shapes our affective and cognitive responses to the film.

Simon Critchley begins by considering the ways in which Malick's film differs from James Jones' book The Thin Red Line, which is its literary source. He cautions against the "hermeneutic banana skin" of taking the film to be an exemplification of philosophical themes grounded in Malick's philosophical training. In the body of his essay, he identifies three key relationships in the film that thematize issues of loyalty (Tall and Staros), love (Bell and his wife), and truth (Witt and Welsh). Focusing on the relationship between Witt and Welsh, he argues that the key to understanding the film lies in the manner in which Witt confronts his death, a manner that echoes the "calm" that Witt ascribes to his own mother, on her deathbed, in an early scene in the film. At the core of The Thin Red Line, Critchley argues, is "this experience of calm in the face of death, of a kind of peace at the moment of one's extinction that is the only place one may speak of immortality." This experience of calm, he maintains, frames the film and, in particular, the character of Welsh, who, while attracted to Witt's "spark," never overcomes his belief that "everything is a lie."

To see why calm is the key to the film and to Malick's art, Critchley examines the film's representation of nature, as "an ineluctable power, a warring force that both frames human war but is utterly indifferent to human purposes and intentions." "Calm," then, is the only proper response to "the fact that human death is absorbed into the relentlessness of nature." Calm is also what lies at the heart of Malick's art, "a calmness to his cinematic eye, a calmness that is also communicated by his films."

Hubert Dreyfus and Camilo Prince argue that The Thin Red Line treats the phenomenon of war as a special case of the violent destruction of "worlds" and the need to confront the phenomenon of "world collapse." In elucidating the notion of "world collapse," they draw upon the Heideggerian distinction between "demise"—death as a terminal biological or ontic phenomenon—and "ontological death"—"world collapse" or the loss of what gives meaning to one's world. Ontological death can befall both individual human beings and a culture. Dreyfus and Prince identify two important differences between demise and ontological death. First, unlike demise, ontological death is something lived through—one can experience "world collapse" only if one remains alive. Second, whereas demise eventually befalls all individuals and cultures, an individual or culture need not experience any form of ontological death during its existence.

Most of the deaths highlighted in the film, Dreyfus and Prince maintain, are cases of ontological death, not of demise, and their chapter focuses on the former. They briefly discuss instances of "cultural collapse" involving the defeated Japanese and the Melanesian villagers, and the "world collapse" that war represents through its destruction of the norms that normally regulate human interaction. The main focus of their essay, however, is on the different ways in which individuals in the film either confront or are invulnerable to "world collapse." They distinguish two ways in which soldiers confront "world collapse"—through "identity failure" and through collapse of an "unconditional commitment." Of greater significance for our understanding of the film, however, are two ways in which individuals can prove invulnerable to "world collapse": first, as with Welsh, through cynical denial of the attempt to make sense of the world, and second, as with Witt, through achieving a "spiritual invulnerability." Unlike his fellow soldiers whose way of life is threatened by their experiences of war, Witt "doesn't form defining commitments nor expect to find meaning, and so does not live in a vulnerable world."

David Davies begins by outlining the astonishing diversity of critical interpretations that have been offered of *The Thin Red Line*, interpretations which fail to agree on even the basic purpose and direction of the film. This, he suggests, is due in part to the structural and thematic complexity of the film, which punctuates its multi-faceted narrative with stream-of-consciousness voiceovers, stunning images of natural beauty, and a haunting musical soundtrack that is interwoven with equally haunting diegetic sounds. In attempting to make sense of this multiplicity of interpretations, he identifies what he takes to be a neglected central theme in the film, through which it not only engages with (without answering) the philosophical questions posed in the dialogic and monologic content, but does so in a uniquely cinematic way, thereby exemplifying the philosophical possibilities of cinema. What commentators have missed, he argues, is the centrality of the visual and the tactile, as inflections of our cognitive engagement with the world in which we act and are acted upon. The film, both thematically and cinematically, offers, through the character of Witt, a model of embodied seeing and embodied agency.

In the final section of his chapter, he examines how the notion of embodied seeing is exemplified in the cinematic style of Malick's film. Malick's images, he argues, have a tactile, holistic quality, the camera representing things in terms of their textures, and acting as a medium of touch as much as of vision. Like Critchley, he also focuses on the role of voiceovers in *The Thin Red Line*. The latter, he argues, present the viewer with a stream of reflective thinking that generally stands apart from the actions of the characters. The voiceovers serve, along with the depictions of nature, as the frame for the human actions presented—actions that are always those of embodied agents whose embodied actions, while called forth by the experienced world, are permeated by language and conceptual awareness. In this way, the voiceovers play an essential part in Malick's cinematic presentation of the manner in which the human agent encounters and responds to his or her world.

Amy Coplan examines the relationship between formal features of *The Thin Red Line* and the emotional, affective, and perceptual experiences the film evokes. While it is characteristic of the cinematic medium in general that it can create stories through the selective presentation of visual and aural information, Malick's films, she argues, are more cinematic than most because they foreground features of experience that can only be communicated through appeal to the senses.

The cinematic style of *The Thin Red Line*, she maintains, is highly unconventional compared to standard Hollywood cinema. Two effects of this style are that much of viewers' affective experience of the film is non-cognitive or minimally cognitive, and that viewers' perception and attention are often focused on sensory information. Coplan provides a detailed analysis of various filmmaking techniques that Malick and his cinematographer used to construct an episodic narrative and to create numerous shots, scenes, and sequences that are highly subjective and impressionistic. Three distinctive formal features of the film—a highly subjective perspective, impressionistic images and sounds, and an episodic narrative—result in viewers having an overall emotional or affective experience of the film that is, at least initially, primarily perceptual and embodied rather than cognitive and evaluative. This analysis helps to show how particular aesthetic characteristics are created during the process of filmmaking and how cinematic techniques through cinematic style influence audience response.

Coplan argues that Malick's film directly engages the senses and elicits more non-cognitive affects than traditional films because of specific ways in which it presents information. For example, the opening sequence of *The Thin Red Line* organizes the narrative episodically and presents much of it from a subjective perspective. As a result, our response to the opening of the film is more experiential than intellectual. She also discusses the cinematography of the film, and the ways in which the camera movement contributes to the creation of a subjective perspective. Finally, she considers the contribution of the lighting techniques used in *The Thin Red Line* to the film's formal style and some of the ways in which this influences viewers' experience.

Iain Macdonald uses Malick's most recent film, *The New World*, to explore in more detail a question raised by Critchley, namely the manner in which nature is represented in Malick's cinema. Macdonald maintains that the specific quality of human participation in nature—the nature of the "war in the heart of nature" thematized in the opening sequence of *The Thin Red Line*—is the central concern of Malick's cinema, but that, while Malick's films show us the power and indifference of nature, we need to inquire further as to the metaphysics that underlies this view. *The New World* provides the occasion for pushing these reflections further because, beyond the conflicts that define the history of the interaction of the two cultures in the film, there is a deeper identity at work, a human identity in reason. The strength of the film, however, is that it does not stop with the idea of a common humanity. The question is rather what *drives* this common reason. It is, Macdonald claims, a question of origins and, more specifically, a question of the relation of human reason to blind nature. If Malick's films attest to a "community of being" that transcends the distinction between human and non-human, then the coherence of this community beyond all communities depends upon what sustains it.

Answering these questions, Macdonald argues, requires making Malick's metaphysics clear. It is, he claims, a materialism, roughly Nietzschean in character, that denies not just cultural essentialism, but also any meaningful distinction between reason and nature. The end result is that the seemingly human capacity of reason turns out to be

nothing more than an expression of the "blind" rationality of nature—
not an exception to the rule of nature but its unqualified realization.
All is struggle and conflict, a "war in the heart of nature," but one in
which human beings play no special role, in spite of what we might
think. It is just that we have the capacity to see this war for what it is.
Strictly speaking, there are no perspectives "on" nature that escape
the natural character of generating such perspectives. This, ultimately,
for Macdonald, is what Malick seems to be telling us. Human self-
understanding, the narratives we tell ourselves, and even the individuality
of cultures and people, are all parasitical upon the obscure becoming of
nature, or what Nietzsche called the "will to power"—the real "war" in
the heart of nature.

References

Bersani, L. and Dutoit, U. (2004) Forms of Being: Cinema, Aesthetics, Subjectivity,
    London: British Film Institute Publishing, 124–78.
Campbell, N. (2003) "The Highway Kind: Badlands, Youth, Space and the Road,"
    in H. Patterson, ed. (2003), 37–49.
Chion, M. (2004) The Thin Red Line, London: British Film Institute Publishing.
Flanagan, M. (2003) "'Everything a Lie': the Critical and Commercial Reception
    of Terrence Malick's The Thin Red Line," in Patterson, ed. (2003), 123–36.
McGettigan, J. (2003) "Days of Heaven and the Myth of the West," in Patterson,
    ed. (2003), 50–60.
Martin, A. (2008) Terrence Malick, London: British Film Institute Publishing.
Morrison, J. and Schur, T. (2003) The Films of Terrence Malick, London: Praeger.
Orr, J. (1998) Contemporary Cinema, Edinburgh: Edinburgh University Press.
—— (2003) "Terrence Malick and Arthur Penn: The Western Re-Myth," in
    Patterson, ed. (2003), 61–74.
Patterson, H. (ed.) (2003) The Cinema of Terrence Malick: Poetic Visions of America,
    London: Wallflower Press.
—— (ed.) (2007) The Cinema of Terrence Malick: Poetic Visions of America, 2nd expanded
    edn, London: Wallflower Press.

Chapter 2

Simon Critchley

CALM—ON TERRENCE MALICK'S
THE THIN RED LINE[1]

Life contracts and death is expected,
As in a season of autumn.
The soldier falls.

He does not become a three-days personage,
Imposing his separation,
Calling for pomp.

Death is absolute and without memorial,
As in a season of autumn,
When the wind stops,

When the wind stops and, over the heavens,
The clouds go, nevertheless,
In their direction.

Wallace Stevens, "The Death of a Soldier"

WITTGENSTEIN ASKS A QUESTION, which sounds like the first line of a joke: How does one philosopher address another? To which the unfunny and perplexing riposte is, "Take your time" (Wittgenstein 1980: 80). Terrence Malick is evidently someone who takes his time. Since his first movie, *Badlands*, was premiered at the New York Film Festival in 1973, he has directed just three more: *Days of Heaven*, in 1979, and then nearly a twenty-year gap until the long-awaited 1998 movie, The Thin Red Line, followed in 2006 by The New World.

The Thin Red Line is a war film. It deals with the events surrounding the battle for Guadalcanal in November 1942, as the US Army fought its bloody way north across the islands of the South Pacific against ferocious Japanese resistance. But it is a war film in the same way that Homer's Iliad is a war poem. The viewer seeking verisimilitude and documentation of historical fact will be disappointed. Rather, Malick's movie is a story of what we might call "heroic fact": of death, of fate, of pointed and pointless sacrifice. Finally, it is a tale of love, both erotic love and, more importantly, the love of compassion whose cradle is military combat and whose greatest fear is dishonor. In one nighttime scene, we see Captain Staros in close-up praying, "Let me not betray my men."

The ambition of The Thin Red Line is unapologetically epic, the scale is not historical but mythical, and the language is lyrical, even at times metaphysical. At one point in the film, Colonel Tall, the commanding officer of the campaign, cites a Homeric epithet about "rosy-fingered dawn," and confesses to the Greek-American Staros that he read the Iliad in Greek while a student at West Point military academy—Staros himself speaks Greek on two occasions. Like the Iliad, Malick deals with the huge human themes by focusing not on a whole war, and not even with an overview of a whole battle, but on the lives of a group of individuals—C-for-Charlie company—in a specific aspect of a battle over the period of a couple of weeks.

To non-Americans—and perhaps to many contemporary Americans as well—the significance of Guadalcanal might not be familiar. It was the key battle in the war against Japan, in a campaign that led from the attack on Pearl Harbor in 1941 to American victory and post-war imperial hegemony. If we cast the Japanese in the role of the Trojans, and Guadalcanal in the place of Troy, then The Thin Red Line might be said to recount the pre-history of American empire in the same way as Homer recites the pre-history of Hellenic supremacy. It might be viewed as a founding myth, and like all such myths, from Homer to Virgil to Milton, it shows both the necessity for an enemy in the act of founding and the often uncanny intimacy with that enemy. Some of the most haunting images of the film are those in which members of Charlie company sit face-to-face with captured Japanese soldiers surrounded by corpses, mud, and the dehumanizing detritus of battle.

Malick based his screenplay on James Jones's five hundred-page 1963 novel The Thin Red Line (Jones 1998b). Jones served as an infantryman in the US Army in the South Pacific, and The Thin Red Line, though fictional, is extensively based on Jones's wartime experiences. Jones was following the formula he established in his first book, the nine hundred-page, 1952 raw blockbuster From Here to Eternity (Jones 1998a), which deals with events surrounding the bombing of Pearl Harbor. A highly expurgated version of From Here to Eternity, starring Burt Lancaster, Deborah Kerr, Montgomery Clift, and Frank Sinatra, won the Academy Award for Best Motion Picture in 1953. Malick's movie won just one Oscar, to Hans Zimmer, for Best Original Score.

A curious fact to note about Malick's The Thin Red Line is that it is a remake. Jones's book was turned into a movie directed by Andrew Marton and starring Keir Dullea and Jack Warden in 1964. This is a low-budget, technically clumsy, averagely acted, and indeed slightly saucy movie, where the jungles of the South Pacific have been replanted in Spain, where the picture was shot. But it is a good honest picture, and there are many analogues with Malick's version, particularly the dialogues between Colonel Tall and Captain Stein.

The narrative focus of the 1964 picture is on Private Doll who is an independently minded existentialist rebel, closer to a young Brando than Albert Camus, who discovers himself in the heat of battle through killing "Japs." The guiding theme is the insanity of war, the thin red line between the sane and the mad, and we are offered a series of more or less trite reflections on the meaninglessness of war. Yet, in this respect, the 1964 film is much more faithful to James Jones's 1963 novel than Malick's treatment, with its more metaphysical intimations. In the 1964 movie, the existential hero finds himself through the act of killing. War is radical meaninglessness, but it is that in relation to which meaning can be given to an individual life. Doll eventually crosses the thin red line and goes crazy, killing everyone in sight, including his own comrades.

The novel is a piece of tough-minded and earnest Americana, somewhere between fiction and reportage, that at times brilliantly evokes the exhausting and dehumanizing pointlessness of war. The book's great virtue is its evocation of camaraderie, the physical and emotional intensity of the relations between the men in C-for-Charlie company. Some of the characters are finely and fully drawn, in particular Fife, Doll, and Bell, but I don't think it is too severe to say that James Jones is not James Joyce. Yet, in this regard, the novel serves Malick's purposes extremely well because it provides him with the raw narrative prime matter from which to form his screenplay. For example, the central protagonist of Malick's version, Witt, brilliantly played by Jim Caviezel, is a more marginal figure in Jones's novel. He drifts repeatedly in and out of the action, having been transferred from Charlie company to Cannon company, which is a collection of brigands and reprobates, but he is eventually readmitted to Charlie company because of his exceptional valor in battle. He is depicted as a stubborn, single-minded, half-educated troublemaker from Breathitt County, Kentucky, motivated by racism, a powerful devotion to his comrades, and an obscure ideal of honor. Although there is an essential solitude to Witt's character that must have appealed to Malick, the latter transforms him into a much more angelic, self-questioning, philosophical figure. Indeed, the culminating action of Malick's film is Witt's death, which does not even occur in the novel, where he is shown at the end of the book finally reconciled with Fife, his former buddy. Fife is the central driving character of Jones's novel, together with Doll, Bell, and Welsh. I have been informed that Malick shot about seven hours of film, but had to cut it to three hours to meet his contract. Therefore, the whole story of Fife—and doubtless much else—was cut out. Other of Malick's characters are inventions, like Captain Staros, the Greek who takes the place of the Jewish Captain Stein. And, interestingly, there are themes in the novel that Malick does not take up, such as the homosexual relations between comrades, in particular Doll's emerging acknowledgment of his homosexuality.

It would appear that Malick has a very free relation to his material. But appearances can be deceptive. For Jones, there was a clear thematic and historical continuity between From Here to Eternity and The Thin Red Line and Malick respects that continuity by integrating passages and characters from the former book into his screenplay. For example, the character of Colonel Tall is lifted from the earlier novel and, more importantly, Prewitt in From Here To Eternity becomes fused with Witt, becoming literally pre-Witt. As Jimmie E. Cain has shown in an invaluable article, Prewitt's speculations about his mother's death and the question of immortality are spoken by Witt in the important opening scenes of The Thin Red Line. After Malick repeatedly consulted Gloria Jones, the late novelist's wife, about the slightest changes from novel to screenplay, she apparently remarked, "Terry, you have my husband's voice, you're writing in his musical key; now what you must do is improvise. Play riffs on this" (cited in Cain 2000).

Malick crafts the matter of Jones's work into a lyrical, economical, and highly wrought screenplay. While there are many memorable passages of dialogue, and some extraordinarily photographed extended action sequences, the core of the film is carried by Malick's favourite cinematic technique: the voiceover. This is worth considering in some detail, for, as Michael Filippidis (2000) has argued, the voiceover provides the entry point for all three of Malick's films. In *Badlands*, the voiceovers are provided by Holly (Sissy Spacek), and in *Days of Heaven* by the child Linda (Linda Manz). The technique of the voiceover allows the character to assume a distance from the cinematic action and a complicity with the audience, an intimate distance that is meditative, ruminative, at times speculative. It is like watching a movie with someone whispering into your ear.

If the technique of the voiceover is common to all three films, then what changes in *The Thin Red Line*, is the subject of the narration. *Badlands* and *Days of Heaven* are narrated from a female perspective and it is through the eyes of two young, poorly educated women that we are invited to view the world. In *The Thin Red Line*, the voiceovers are male and plural. The only female characters are the wife of Bell who appears in dream sequences and whose only words are "Come out. Come out where I am"; the young Melanesian mother that Witt meets at the beginning of the film; and the recollected scene of Witt's mother's deathbed. Although it is usually possible to identify the speaker of the voiceover, their voices sometimes seem to blend into one another, particularly during the closing scenes of the film when the soldiers are leaving Guadalcanal on board a landing craft. As the camera roams from face to face, almost drunkenly, the voices become one voice, one soul, "as if all men got one big soul"—but we will come back to this.

The Thin Red Line is words with music. The powerful effect of the voiceovers cannot be distinguished from that of the music which accompanies them. The score, which bears sustained listening on its own account, was composed by Hans Zimmer, who collaborated extensively with Malick. The latter's use of music in his movies is at times breathtaking, and the structure of his films bears a close relation to musical composition, where leitmotifs function as both punctuation and recapitulation of the action—a technique Malick employed to great effect in *Days of Heaven*. In all three of his movies, there is a persistent presence of natural sounds, particularly flowing water and birdsong. The sound of the breeze in the vast fields of ripening wheat in *Days of Heaven* finds a visual echo in what was the most powerful memory I had from my first viewing of *The Thin Red Line*: the sound of the wind and soldiers' bodies moving through the Kunai grass as Charlie company ascend the hill towards the enemy position. Nature appears as an impassive and constant presence that frames human conflict.

Three hermeneutic banana skins

There are a number of hermeneutic banana skins that any study of Malick's art can slip up on, particularly when the critic is a philosopher. Before turning more directly to the film, let me take my time to discuss three of them.

First, there is what we might call the paradox of privacy. Malick is clearly a very private person who shuns publicity. This is obviously no easy matter in the movie business and in this regard Malick invites comparison with Kubrick who, by contrast, appears a paragon of productivity. Of course, the relative paucity of biographical data on Malick simply feeds a curiosity of the most trivial and quotidian kind. I must confess to this curiosity myself, but I do not think it should be sated. There should be no speculation, then, on "the enigmatic Mr Malick," or whatever.

But if one restricts oneself to the biographical information that I have been able to find out, then a second banana skin appears in one's path, namely the intriguing issue of Malick and philosophy. He studied philosophy at Harvard University between 1961 and 1965, graduating with Phi Beta Kappa honors. He worked closely with Stanley Cavell, who supervised Malick's undergraduate honors thesis. Against the deeply ingrained prejudices about Continental thought that prevailed at that time, Malick courageously attempted to show how Heidegger's thoughts about (and against) epistemology in *Being and Time* could be seen in relation to the analysis of perception in Russell, Moore and, at Harvard, C.I. Lewis. Malick then went, as a Rhodes scholar, to Magdalen College, Oxford, to study for the B.Phil in philosophy. He left Oxford because he wanted to write a D.Phil thesis on the concept of world in Kierkegaard, Heidegger, and Wittgenstein, and was told by Gilbert Ryle that he should try to write on something more "philosophical." He then worked as a philosophy teacher at MIT, teaching Hubert Dreyfus's course on Heidegger when he was away on study leave in France, and wrote journalism for *The New Yorker* and *Life* magazine. In 1969, he published his bilingual edition of Heidegger's *Vom Wesen des Grundes* as *The Essence of Reasons* (Heidegger 1969). Also in 1969, he was accepted into the inaugural class of the Center for Advanced Film Studies at the American Film Institute in Los Angeles, and his career in cinema began to take shape.

Clearly, then, Malick's is a highly sophisticated, philosophically trained intellect. Yet the young philosopher decided not to pursue an academic career, but to pass from philosophy to film, for reasons that remain obscure. Given these facts, it is extremely tempting—almost overwhelmingly so—to read through his films to some philosophical pretext or metatext, to interpret the action of his characters in Heideggerian, Wittgensteinian or, indeed, Cavellian terms. To make matters worse, Malick's movies seem to make philosophical statements and present philosophical positions. Nonetheless, to read through the cinematic image to some identifiable philosophical master text would be a mistake, for it would be not to read at all.

So, what is the philosopher to do faced with Malick's films? This leads me to a third hermeneutic banana skin. To read from cinematic language to some philosophical metalanguage is both to miss what is specific to the medium of film and usually to engage in some sort of cod-philosophy deliberately designed to intimidate the uninitiated. I think this move has to be avoided on philosophical grounds, indeed the very best Heideggerian grounds. Any philosophical reading of film has to be a reading of film, of what Heidegger would call *der Sache selbst*, the thing itself. A philosophical reading of film should not be concerned with ideas about the thing, but with the thing itself, the cinematic *Sache*. It seems to me that a consideration of Malick's art demands that we take seriously the idea that film is less an illustration of philosophical ideas and theories—let's call that a *philoso-fugal* reading—and more a form of philosophizing, of reflection, reasoning, and argument. (For a similar line of argument on the relation of philosophy to film, see Mulhall 2002.)

Loyalty, love, and truth

Let me now turn to the film itself. The narrative of *The Thin Red Line* is organized around three relationships, each composed of a conflict between two characters. The first relationship is that between Colonel Tall, played by Nick Nolte, and Captain Staros, played by Elias Koteas. At the core of this relationship is the question of loyalty, a conflict between loyalty to the commands of one's superiors and loyalty to the men under one's command. This relationship comes to a crisis when Staros refuses a direct order from Tall to lead an attack on a machinegun position of the Japanese. Staros says: "I've lived with these men for two and a half years, and I will not order them to their deaths"—for the carnage that the Japanese are causing from their superior hilltop vantage point and the scenes of slaughter are truly awful. Suppressing his fury, Tall goes up the line to join Charlie company and skilfully organizes a flanking assault on the Japanese position. After the successful assault, he gives Staros a humiliating lecture about the necessity of allowing one's men to die in battle. He decides that Staros is not tough-minded enough to lead his men and, after recommending him for the Silver Star and the Purple Heart, immediately relieves him of his commission and orders him back to a desk job in Washington DC. Loyalty to the men under one's command must be subservient to the pragmatics of the battlefield.

The second relationship, based on love, is that between Private Bell (Ben Chaplin) and his wife Marty (Miranda Otto), and is dealt with rather abstractly by Malick. It is much more central to the 1964 version of the film, where it is transposed into the relationship between Private Doll and one "Judy." In Jones's novel, Bell is a former army officer who had been a First Lieutenant in the Philippines. He and his wife had an extraordinarily close, intense relationship ("We were always very sexual together," he confesses to Fife), and after spending four months separated from his wife in the jungle, he decided that he'd had enough and resigned his commission. As retribution, the US Army said that they would make sure he was drafted, and, moreover, drafted into the infantry as a private. All that we see of the relationship in the film, however, are a series of dream images of Bell with Marty, what Jones calls "weird transcendental images of Marty's presence." Then, after the battle, we hear Bell reading a letter from his wife saying that she has left him for an Air Force captain.

After the failures of loyalty and love, the theme of truth is treated in the third relationship, and this is what I would like to concentrate on. The characters here are Sergeant Welsh, played with consummate craft by Sean Penn, and Private Witt. The question at issue here is metaphysical truth; or, more precisely, whether there is such a thing as metaphysical truth. Baldly stated: is this the only world, or is there another world? The conflict is established in the first dialogue between the two soldiers, after Witt has been incarcerated for going AWOL in a Melanesian village, in the scenes of somewhat cloying communal harmony that open the film. Welsh says, "in this world, a man himself is nothing . . . and there ain't no world but this one." To which Witt replies, "You're wrong there, I seen another world. Sometimes I think it's just my imagination." And Welsh completes the thought: "Well, you're seeing something I never will."

Welsh is a sort of physicalist egoist who is contemptuous of everything. Jones writes:

> Everything amused Welsh . . . Politics amused him, religion amused him, particularly ideals and integrity amused him; but most of all human virtue amused him. He did not believe in it and did not believe in any of those other words.
>
> Jones 1998b: 24

Behind this complete moral nihilism, the only thing in which Welsh believes is property. He refuses to let Staros commend him for a Silver Star after an act of extraordinary valor in which he dodged hails of bullets to give morphine to a buddy dying on the battlefield, and quips: "Property, the whole fucking thing's about property." War is fought for property, one nation against another nation. The war is taking place in service of a lie, the lie of property. You either believe the lie or you die, like Witt. Welsh says—and it is a sentiment emphasized in the book and both versions of the film—"Everything is a lie. Only one thing a man can do, find something that's his, make an island for himself." It is only by believing that, and shutting his eyes to the bloody lie of war, that he can survive. Welsh's physicalism is summarized in the phrase that in many ways guides the 1964 version of the film and which appears briefly in Malick: "It's only meat." The human being is meat and only this belief both exposes the lie and allows one to survive—and Welsh survives.

Facing Welsh's nihilistic physicalism is what we might call Witt's Emersonian metaphysical panpsychism, caught in the question, "Maybe all men got one big soul, that everybody's a part of—all faces are the same man, one big self." Witt is the questioner, the contemplator, the mystic, perhaps even the holy fool. Much of what he says is in the form of questions—the very piety of thinking for Heidegger—and not the assertions propounded by Welsh. Unflinchingly brave in combat, with absolutely no thought of his own safety and prepared to sacrifice himself for his comrades, Witt views all things and persons with an impassive constancy, and sees beauty and goodness in all things. Where Welsh sees only the pain caused by human selfishness, Witt looks at the same scenes and feels the glory. He is like a redemptive angel looking into the souls of soldiers and seizing hold of their spark. It is this metaphysical commitment that fuels both Witt's selfless courage in combat and his compassion for the enemy. In one of the most moving scenes of the film, he looks into the face of a dead Japanese soldier, half-buried in the dirt—which speaks to him with a prophecy of his own fate—"Are you loved by all? Know that I was. Do you imagine that your sufferings will be less because you loved goodness, truth?" In their final dialogue, Witt says that he still sees a spark in Sergeant Welsh. The truth is, I think, that Welsh is half in love with Witt, and behind his nihilism there is a grudging but total respect for Witt's commitment. Welsh cannot believe what Witt believes, he cannot behold the glory. And yet, he is also unable to feel nothing, to feel numb to the suffering that surrounds him. As a consequence, he is in profound pain. In tears, at the foot of Witt's grave, Welsh asks, "Where's your spark now?," which might as well be a question to himself.

As in the two other relationships, there seems to be a clear winner and loser. As Welsh predicts in their second dialogue, the reward for Witt's metaphysical commitment will be death. Loyalty to one's men leads to dismissal from one's position, loyalty in love leads to betrayal, and loyalty to a truth greater than oneself leads to death. Yet, Malick is too intelligent to make didactic art. Truth consists in the conflict, or series of conflicts, between positions; and in watching those conflicts unravel, we are instructed, deepened. This conflict is particularly clear in the depiction of war itself. For this is not simply an anti-war film and has none of the post-adolescent bombast of Francis Ford Coppola's *Apocalypse Now* (1979), the cloying self-righteousness of Oliver Stone's *Platoon* (1986), or the gnawing, sentimental nationalism of *Saving Private Ryan* (1998). One of the voiceovers states, "War don't ennoble men. It turns them into dogs. Poisons the soul." But this view has to be balanced with a central message of the film: namely, that there is a total risk of the self in battle, an utter emptying of the self, that does not produce egoism, but rather a powerful bond of compassionate love for one's comrades and even for one's enemy. The inhumanity of war lets one see through the fictions of a people, a tribe or a nation towards a common humanity. The imponderable question is why it should require such suffering to bring us to this recognition.

Immortality

I would like to stay a little longer with the character of Witt and consider in detail one scene from the movie, namely the instant of his death. Witt, like all the male protagonists from Malick's previous movies, goes to his death with a sense of acceptance, willingness even. In Badlands, Kit (Martin Sheen) desires nothing more than the glorious notoriety of death and we assume at the end of the picture that he is going to be electrocuted. In Days of Heaven, the Farmer (Sam Shepherd) is told by his doctor that he is going to die, and it is this overheard conversation that prompts Bill (Richard Gere) into planning the deception of a marriage with his partner, Abby (Brooke Adams). After Gere stabs Shepherd to death in a smouldering wheatfield, one has the sense that this is exactly what the Farmer desired. Similarly, when Bill is gunned down at the end of Days of Heaven—in an amazing shot photographed from underwater as his face hits the river—one has a powerful intimation of an ineluctable fate working itself out. In short, Malick's male protagonists seem to foresee their appointment with death and endeavor to make sure they arrive on time. Defined by a fatalistic presentiment of their demise, they are all somehow in love with death. Yet, such foreknowledge does not provoke fear and trembling; on the contrary, it brings, I will suggest, a kind of calm.

There is an utter recklessness to Witt and he repeatedly puts himself in situations of extreme danger. He is among the first to volunteer for the small unit that makes the highly dangerous flanking move to destroy the Japanese machinegun position, and the action that leads to his eventual death at the end of the film is very much of his own making. So, to this extent, Witt fits the death-bound pattern of Malick's male protagonists. Yet, what is distinctive about the character of Witt is that at the core of his sense of mortality lies the metaphysical question of immortality. This is established in the opening scenes of the movie in the Melanesian village, when he is shown talking to an unnamed comrade who has also gone AWOL. Against the recollected image of his mother's deathbed (Figure 1), he says:

> I remember my mother when she was dying, all shrunken and grey. I asked if she was afraid. She just shook her head. I was afraid to touch the death that I seen in her. I couldn't find anything beautiful or uplifting about her going back to God. I heard people talk about immortality, but I ain't never seen it.

The point here is that Witt is afraid of the death that descends over his mother, he can't touch it, find any comfort in it, or believe that it is the passage to her immortal home in bliss. Witt is then profiled standing on the beach, and he continues, less sceptically, and this time in a voiceover:

> I wondered how it'd be when I died. What it'd be like to know that this breath now was the last one you was ever gonna draw. I just hope I can meet it the same way she did, with the same . . . calm. Because that's where it's hidden, the immortality that I hadn't seen.

It is this pause between "same" and "calm" that I want to focus on, this breathing space for a last breath. For I think this calm is the key to the film and, more widely, to Malick's art. The metaphysical issue of the reality or otherwise of immortality obviously cannot be settled and that is not the point. The thought here is that the only immortality imaginable

Figure 1

is found in a calm that can descend at the moment of death. The eternal life can only be imagined as inhabiting the instant of one's death, of knowing that this is the last breath that you are going to draw and not being afraid.[2]

With this in mind, let's look at the instant of Witt's death. Charlie Company are making their way, very precariously, up a river, and the whole scene, as elsewhere in Malick, is saturated with the sound of flowing river water. Phone lines back to HQ have been cut, enemy artillery fire is falling all around them and is getting steadily closer. The company is under the command of the peculiarly incompetent Lieutenant Band, who is leading them into an extremely exposed position where they will be sitting ducks for an enemy attack. Rather than retreating, as he should have done, Band hurriedly decides to send a small scouting party up the river to judge the proximity of the enemy. He chooses the terrified Fife and the adolescent Coombs, and then Witt quickly volunteers himself. After progressing a little way up the river, they are seen by the enemy and Coombs is shot, but not fatally wounded. Witt sends Fife back to the company and the wounded Coombs floats back downstream. In an act of complete selflessness, Witt allows himself to be used as a decoy and leads a squad of Japanese soldiers into the jungle. Witt then suddenly finds himself in a small clearing surrounded on all sides by some twenty Japanese troops. Breathless and motionless, he stands still whilst the Japanese squad leader screams at him, presumably demanding that he defend himself. Witt remains stock still, recovers his breath and then realizes that he is going to die. The scene seems agonizingly long, the music slowly builds and there is a slow zoom into Witt's face (Figure 2). He is . . . calm. Then the camera slowly zooms out and there is a brief cutting shot of him half-heartedly raising his gun as he is gunned down. Malick then cuts to images of nature, of trees, water and birds.

What is one to make of this? Obvious philosophical parallels can be drawn here. For example, Heidegger's notion of *Angst* or anxiety is experienced with the presentiment of my mortality, what he calls "being-towards-death." In one famous passage from the 1929 lecture, "What is Metaphysics?," a text that Malick surely knows as it is directly contemporary with *The Essence of Reasons*, Heidegger is anxious to distinguish *Angst* from all sorts of fear and trembling. He says that the experience of *Angst* is a kind of *Ruhe*, peace or calm (Heidegger 1978: 102). Similarly,

Figure 2

in Blanchot's tantalizingly brief memoir, *L'instant de ma mort* (1994), the seemingly autobiographical protagonist is described at the point of being executed by German soldiers, a fate from which he eventually escapes. He describes the feeling as "*un sentiment de légèreté extraordinaire, une sorte de béatitude.*" One also thinks of Wittgenstein's remark from the *Tractatus*, "the eternal life is given to those who live in the present" (Wittgenstein 2004: 6.4311). One could go on amassing examples. To interpret Malick's treatment of death in line with such thoughts is extremely tempting, but it would be to slip up on one or more of those hermeneutic banana skins discussed above. It would be to offer ideas about the thing rather than *der Sache Selbst*.

At the core of *The Thin Red Line*, then, is this experience of calm in the face of death, of a kind of peace at the moment of one's extinction that is the only place one may speak of immortality. This experience of calm frames the film and paradoxically provides the context for the bloody and cruel action of war. In particular, it frames the character of Welsh, who cares for Witt and his "beautiful light" much more than he can admit, but persists to the end of the film in his belief that everything is a lie. His almost final words are, "You're in a box, a moving box. They want you dead or in their lie."

All things shining—the place of nature in Malick

Why do I claim that calm is the key to Malick's art? To try to tease this out, I would like to turn to the theme of nature, whose massive presence

is the constant backdrop to Malick's movies. If calm in t[...]
mortality is the frame for the human drama of The Thin Red Line, th[...]
is the frame for this frame, a power that at times completely oversh[...]
the human drama.

The Thin Red Line opens with the image of a huge crocodile slo[...]
submerging into a weed-covered pond—the crocodile who makes a bri[...]
return appearance towards the end of the film, when it is shown captured
by some men from Charlie company, who prod it abstractedly with a
stick. Against images of jungle trees densely wrapped in suffocating vines,
we hear the first words of the movie, spoken by an unidentified voice:
"What's this war in the heart of nature? Why does nature vie with itself,
the land contend with the sea? Is there an avenging power in nature?
Not one power, but two." Obviously, the war in the heart of nature has
a double meaning, suggesting both a war internal to nature, and the
human war that is being fought out amid such immense natural beauty.
These two meanings are brought together later in the film by Colonel
Tall, when he is in the process of dismissing Staros from his commission and justifying the brutality of war: "Look at this jungle, look at
those vines, the way they twine around the trees, swallowing everything.
Nature is cruel, Staros." Images of trees wrapped in vines punctuate The
Thin Red Line, together with countless images of birds, in particular owls
and parrots. These images are combined with the almost constant
presence of natural sounds, of birdsong, of the wind in the Kunai grass,
of animals moving in the undergrowth, and the sound of water, both
waves lapping on the beach and the flowing of the river.

Nature might be viewed as a kind of fatum for Malick, an ineluctable
power, a warring force that both frames human war but is utterly
indifferent to human purposes and intentions. This beautiful indifference
of nature can be linked to the depiction of nature elsewhere in Malick's
work. For example, Badlands is teeming with natural sounds and images:
with birds, dogs, flowing water, the vast flatness of South Dakota, and
the badlands of Montana, with its mountains in the distance—and always
remaining in the distance. Days of Heaven is also heavily marked with natural
sounds and exquisitely photographed images, with flowing river water,
the wind moving in fields of ripening wheat and silhouetted human
figures working in vast fields. Nature also possesses here an avenging
power, when a plague of locusts descend on the fields and Sam Shepherd
sets fire to an entire wheat crop—nature is indeed cruel.

...ot to grant that nature is playing a symbolic
...animistic conception of nature, of the kind
...ridge's 1802 "Dejection: An Ode": "Oh
...ive/And in our life alone does nature
...ature's indifference to human purposes
...naturalistic conception of nature. Things are
...ck's universe, they simply *are*, and we are things
...ote from us and continue on regardless of our strivings.
...t is suggested by the Wallace Stevens poem cited in the
...ph to this essay. A soldier falls in battle, but his death does not
...vite pomp or transient glory. Rather, death has an absolute character,
which Stevens likens to a moment in autumn when the wind stops. Yet,
when the wind stops, above in the high heavens the clouds continue on
their course, "nevertheless,/In their direction." What is central to Malick,
I think, is this "neverthelessness" of nature, of the fact that human death
is absorbed into the relentlessness of nature, the eternal war in nature
into which the death of a soldier is indifferently ingested. That is where
Witt's spark lies.

There is a calm at the heart of Malick's art, a calmness to his cinematic
eye, a calmness that is also communicated by his films, that becomes the
mood of his audience: after watching *The Thin Red Line* we feel calm. As
Charlie company leave Guadalcanal and are taken back to their ship on a
landing craft, we hear the final voiceover from Witt, this time from
beyond the grave: "Oh my soul, let me be in you now. Look out through
my eyes, look out at the things you made, all things shining." In each of
his movies, one has the sense of things simply being looked at, just being
what they are—trees, water, birds, dogs, crocodiles or whatever. Things
simply are, and are not molded to a human purpose. We watch things
shining calmly, being as they are, in all the intricate evasions of "as." The
camera can be pointed at those things to try to capture some grain or
affluence of their reality. The closing shot of *The Thin Red Line* presents the
viewer with a coconut fallen onto the beach, against which a little water
laps and out of which has sprouted a long green shoot, connoting life,
one imagines. The coconut simply is, it merely lies there remote from us
and our intentions. This suggests to me Stevens's final poem, "The Palm
at the End of the Mind," the palm that simply persists regardless of the
makings of "human meaning." Stevens concludes: "The palm stands on
the edge of space. The wind moves slowly in its branches." In my fancy
at least, I see Malick concurring with this sentiment.

Notes

1 This text was originally prepared to introduce a screening of The Thin Red Line
   at Tate Modern, London, May 2002. It was revised for inclusion in my 2005.
   I mark these dates in order to explain why I say nothing here about Malick's
   The New World (2006). Very sadly, I have come to the view that the less said
   about the latter the better. I would like to thank Nick Bunnin, Stanley Cavell,
   Jim Conant, Hubert Dreyfus, Espen Hammer, Jim Hopkins, and Anne Latto
   for confirming and providing facts about Malick and also for helpful
   comments on my line of argument.

2 What is particularly intriguing is that the passages quoted above are lifted
   from a speech by Prewitt in From Here to Eternity. Jones writes:

   It was hard to accept that he, who was the hub of this known universe, would
   cease to exist, but it was an inevitability and he did not shun it. He only
   hoped that he would meet it with the same magnificent indifference with
   which she who had been his mother met it. Because it was there, he felt,
   that the immortality he had not seen was hidden.

   The question is why Malick replaces "magnificent indifference" with
   "calm." This passage was brought to my attention by Cain 2000: 6.

References

Blanchot, M. (1994) L'instant de ma mort, Montpellier: Fata Morgana.
Cain, J.E. Jr. (2000) "'Writing in his musical key': Terrence Malick's vision of
  The Thin Red Line," Film Criticism, xxv: 2–24.
Critchley, S. (2005) Things Merely Are. Philosophy in the Poetry of Wallace Stevens, London
  and New York: Routledge.
Filippidis, M. (2000) "On Malick's Subjects," Senses of Cinema, www.senses
  ofcinema.com.
Heidegger, M. (1969) The Essence of Reasons, trans. T. Malick, Evanston, IL:
  Northwestern University Press.
—— (1978) "What is Metaphysics?," in D.F. Krell (ed.), Martin Heidegger. Basic
  Writings, London and New York: Routledge.
Jones, J. (1998a) From Here to Eternity, London: Hodder and Stoughton.
—— (1998b) The Thin Red Line, London: Hodder and Stoughton.
Mulhall, S. (2002) On Film, London: Routledge.
Wittgenstein, L. (1980) Culture and Value, trans. P. Winch, Oxford: Blackwell.
—— (2004) Tractatus Logico-Philosophicus, trans. D.F. Pears and B.F. McGuiness,
  London and New York: Routledge.

Chapter 3

Hubert Dreyfus and Camilo Salazar Prince

THE THIN RED LINE: DYING WITHOUT DEMISE, DEMISE WITHOUT DYING

THE THIN RED LINE TREATS THE PHENOMENON of war as a special case of the violent destruction of "worlds" where each soldier must confront the phenomenon of "world collapse" head on in his own distinctive way. Our essay will analyze the journey of some of the soldiers from C-Company as they trudge across the battlefield of Guadalcanal—a world that threatens to bring itself to an end. Before we begin this analysis, however, we must define what we mean by "world collapse" and how it is manifest in the context of war.

Several authors[1] have commented on the importance of the role of death in *The Thin Red Line*. Their arguments turn on the idea that the film is a philosophical investigation into the nature of death and how each individual has to face his own end. Although we consider this to be true, we differ from previous authors in the way we view how death is treated in the film. The main focus of previous work on the subject is solely on the role of death as a terminal biological or ontic phenomenon, what Heidegger terms "demise." For Heidegger, terminal death "is something distinctively impending" (Heidegger 1962: 294), an event that will one day overtake each of us. But ontological death as Heidegger understands it is "a way to be" (ibid.: 245). It is a way of living that takes account of our constant vulnerability to the collapse of our way of life. Most of the deaths in the film are not cases of demise but of the loss of what gives meaning to one's world. Therefore, in discussing *The Thin Red Line*, we feel that we must focus on ontological death, not ontic demise. The ways of dying we are interested in are the sort that can befall individual human beings in cases of world collapse such as identity failure, and that can befall a culture or a cultural epoch in cases such as being taken over by a culture with an alien cultural style (for a striking example, see Lear 2007). We are interested in two important differences between demise and all existential ontological ways of dying.

First, unlike demise, an existential breakdown is lived through. One can only experience world collapse if one remains alive. In other words the individual or culture that undergoes the experience must continue to exist for such a death to occur; what remains after an existential collapse of a human life, which Heidegger calls "being-in-the-world," is more than just a corpse.

Second, an individual or culture need not experience any form of existential breakdown during their existence, that is to say an individual need not experience the loss of his or her identity, and the members of a community need not experience the collapse of their way of life in their lifetime.

Cultural collapse

The Thin Red Line depicts the battle of Guadalcanal as a collision of different cultural worlds on a single battlefield. A vulnerability to cultural collapse is depicted throughout the film through the experiences of war that the Japanese, Americans, and Melanesians endure. The sequence of events that result from the assault on the Japanese camp, for instance, exemplifies the sort of cultural death that threatens the Japanese soldiers. When the soldiers from C-Company storm into the camp, the Japanese, outnumbered and surrounded, respond to the attack in a suicidal manner. While some confront the American soldiers head on and meet with a brutal death, others kneel down and commit hara-kiri, and others meditate amidst the bloodshed. Although death takes the form of violent physical demise in the attack, the final image we see after the carnage is not that of a soldier dying in agony but that of a Buddha being slowly consumed by fire. Although the whole of Japanese culture was not annihilated in this encounter, it was threatened, or better yet the war was a constant threat to the Japanese way of life throughout the war's duration and beyond.

A more vulnerable "world" whose entire existence both as a way of life and as a specific group of human beings is more at risk than any other depicted in the film, is the Melanesian village that we see as a paradise at the beginning of the film when Witt is AWOL. In Witt's second encounter with the Melanesians we realize how truly fragile they are. His eyes disclose to us how they suffer from disease and inner conflicts, but moreover that a war such as the one that is taking place so close to their home is an actual threat that could potentially wipe them out. The fear the Melanesians exude on Witt's second visit is not the same fear the young Melanesian woman expresses with a smile on the first encounter:

Witt:	Are you afraid of me?
Woman:	Yes.
Witt:	Why?
Woman:	Cos you look . . . You look as an army!
Witt:	I look army?
Woman:	Yes.

The later fear is of another sort, a fear deeply rooted in the realization of a danger that the war inflicts on them, the threat of possible annihilation of their village and their way of life. It is through their fear of Witt that we realize that their paradise, just as our world, is not exempt both from physical destruction and from cultural devastation.

World collapse

The existential ontological breakdown of the members of C-Company unfolds as they get closer and closer to the enemy entrenched on Hill 210. The transformation of the battlefield into a groundless world is witnessed by several of the soldiers amidst the chaos. "I got 'em! I got 'em.—I killed a man, nobody can touch me for it," yells Private Doll after shooting a Japanese soldier coming over a ridge. At the moment of the soldier's death Doll realizes he has murdered more than just one man; the normative structure of the world as he knows it has ceased to exist. An exchange between Captain Staros and Lieutenant Colonel Tall further depicts war as world collapse. Tall says: "Now, I know you're a goddamn lawyer! This is not a court of law. This is a war. It's a goddamn battle!"

At a world's end, the starry sky above and the moral law within vanish into thin air, giving way to groundlessness.

The members of C-Company fight in this lawless and groundless world that Tall and Doll describe, and each, in his own way, copes with it. We will proceed by analyzing two ways in which soldiers confront the phenomenon of "world collapse": through identity failure and the collapse of an unconditional commitment; and two ways in which they are invulnerable to it: through cynical denial that the world ever made sense and through achieving spiritual immortality.

Identity failure

In cases of complete existential ontological breakdown an individual's world fully collapses; the light that shed meaning on his or her life suddenly becomes dim and madness lurks in its place. Such a collapse of an individual's world occurs when a person can no longer cope with things in the way one would normally cope with them. Heidegger equates this sort of breakdown with an anxiety attack in which human beings lose their ability to act at all.

There are several cases of this sort of ontological breakdown. The most striking is the case of Sgt McCron, who has just lost all the men in his unit. Surrounded by the men of C-Company before the taking of Hill 210, he grabs a handful of dirt and tells them "this is what we are . . . we're just dirt, we're just dirt." He looks at the dirt in his hand thoughtfully and lets it drift away into the blades of grass that imprison the men. The men trot into battle. McCron remains pensive. Further along in the film, we meet up with McCron a second time and see him walking alone at the top of a hill at sundown screaming his heart out at the senseless space that once was a world: "Look at me! I stand right up here and not one bullet. Not one shot! I can stand right here, I can stand right up and nothing happens to me!" In this case of "world collapse," madness makes McCron at least temporarily invulnerable even to demise.

Unconditional commitment

Two soldiers from C-Company strive to avert world collapse by holding on to a commitment with what Kierkegaard calls "infinite passion" so that it determines their identity and guides their actions through the battle. Captain Staros has a familial commitment to the men he leads, and Private Bell has a passionate commitment of love for his beautiful young wife. For both soldiers, holding on to their unconditional commitment is what ultimately determines their fate on the battleground.

Staros shows his devotion to his men when, in an attempt to save their lives, he disobeys a direct order from his superior, Lt Col Tall, to execute a frontal attack:

Tall: Now, attack, Staros! That's a direct order!
Staros: Sir, I must tell you that I refuse to obey your order.
Tall: Now, I want that frontal attack. I repeat my order. Over.
Staros: Colonel, I refuse to take my men up there in a frontal
            attack. It's suicide, sir. I've lived with these men for two
            years, and I will not order them all to their deaths.

Staros's decision to disobey a direct order as result of his unconditional commitment to his men saves their lives. His prayer, "Let me not betray you. Let me not betray my men," is answered. But once they return to the camp after Hill 210 is taken, Lt Col Tall immediately relieves Staros of his command on the grounds that he is "too soft-hearted." Before Staros is put on a plane to return home his soldiers pay him a visit. They thank him for refusing to obey Tall's order, for "watching out for them, keeping them together." His soldiers feel he got a "rotten deal," they offer to file a complaint. But Staros refuses their help, and says that although he is leaving, they will always be a part of him: "You've been like my sons, you are my sons, my dear sons, you live inside me now, I'll carry you wherever I go." Staros has experienced world collapse but has avoided despair by converting his defining commitment to his men into an idealized memory that no longer relates to the real world.[2]

Private Jack Bell's inner monologues with his wife—"We together. One being. Flow together like water. Till I can't tell you from me. I drink you."—and his sensual remembrances of her show us how devoted he is to their love. More importantly they show how committed he is to surviving the war, and returning "changeless" to her arms: "My dear wife, you get something twisted out of your insides by all this blood, filth, and noise. I want to stay changeless for you. I want to come back to you the man I was before."

Bell is not only seeking physical survival but existential survival as well; he seeks to remain whole in order not to lose the love that defines who he is and what is essential in his world. Faced with the groundlessness of war, with the immediate threat of world collapse, Bell finds his salvation in a love he believes nothing can destroy: "Love. Where does it come from? Who lit this flame in us? No war can put it out, conquer it." His entire life as a man and as soldier is conditioned by his commitment to his wife, the love he feels for her gives him the courage and grounding he needs to survive the war at every level: "Why should I be afraid to die? I belong to you." Although his unconditional commitment to his wife helps him survive the war, as soon as he reaches the camp he must face the destruction of his defining commitment. His wife writes: "Dear Jack, I've met an Air Force captain. I've fallen in love with him. I want a divorce to marry him. Forgive me. Oh, my friend of all those shining years. Help me leave you!" We next see Jack Bell laughing nervously with his wife's letter in hand, his mind spinning in a void of meaninglessness, a greater suffering than demise. We last see him sitting alone, looking completely devastated.

Cynical invulnerability

For a materialist, there is "no world but this one," and this world consists of a set of facts that, although infinite in number, are all potentially discoverable via the wonders of science and reason. There is no place for a spiritual perspective on the world. The world is in essence a collection of spiritless things that humanity attempts to understand rationally and control.

First, Sergeant Welsh resists the perils of war by clinging to a cynical materialist perspective on the world. He says to Witt: "We're living in a world that's blown itself to hell as fast as everybody can arrange it. In a situation like that all a man can do is shut his eyes and let nothing touch him. Look out for himself." To Welsh the world is populated with rocks, dying birds, islands, property, and lies. He lives in a world where "if you die, it's gonna be for nothing" because "there's not some other world out there where everything's gonna be okay. There's just this world. Just this rock." Welsh's invulnerability is his most precious possession, an island he has made for himself, which he is not prepared to give up for anything or anyone. To his mind the war "is about property," a violent scheme that needlessly puts the lives of men at risk in order for a nation to accumulate more and more material possessions, more and more power. Welsh's senseless "world" is built on the rock-solid foundations of nihilism, and unlike all the previous cases we have looked at, Welsh is ontologically invulnerable to "world collapse" because he has no meaningful world that can collapse. He is vulnerable only to demise.

Throughout the film Welsh insists that we are "alone" in the world, that when the world is bringing itself to an end the only thing a soldier can do is shut his eyes and look out for himself and only himself. Yet, despite Welsh's proclaimed self-centeredness and his continual nihilistic remarks, he does not always do as he preaches, that is to say his actions are at times at odds with his words. In the heat of battle, Sergeant Welsh runs across a bullet-ridden field to get morphine to a dying soldier. Staros approaches him, and says: "I saw the whole thing . . . I'm gonna recommend you for the Silver Star. It's the most courageous thing . . ." But before Staros can even finish his sentence Welsh cuts him off: "Captain, if you say one more thing to thank me, I'm going to knock you right in the teeth. If you mention me in your fucking orders, I'll resign my rating so fast and leave you here to run this busted-up outfit all by yourself."

Is Welsh contradicting himself by easing a dying soldier's pain? Does he actually only care about himself? Although his actions seem to be in contradiction with his words, there is nothing contradictory about the way in which Welsh responds to the situation; in fact, it goes hand in hand with his invulnerability to world collapse. He is free to act not because the meaning of his world is secure, but because he has no world that can collapse but only a rock. In rejecting Staros's recommendation for the Silver Star, Welsh is not denying what he did, rather he is rejecting any sort of "worldly" recognition from the "anyone" that fuels the war he is trapped in. The action is consistent with his worldview. By rejecting Staros's recommendation, Welsh is rejecting the "lie" he is fighting in, and therefore not acting in contradiction to what he believes. The act of risking his life to ease the soldier's pain shows he has nothing to lose. He is invulnerable. Welsh is secure in the confines of cynicism, not even demise itself can destroy him. Even if Welsh had been mortally wounded as he ran across the menacing blades of Kunai grass he would have suffered demise without ever dying.

Even though Welsh's cynical perspective makes him invulnerable to world collapse it does not exempt him from feeling pain or having empathy for others. Consider the moment after Hill 210 has been taken. Staring at a dying soldier, Private Storm says, "I look at that boy dying, I don't feel nothing. I don't care about nothing anymore." Welsh replies with absolute honesty: "Sounds like bliss." Like any other human being, Welsh must battle with the emotions that arise when he is confronted with the feelings and thoughts of individuals who have different and sometimes opposing worldviews. In an empty roofless house in the middle of nowhere, Witt asks Welsh: "You care about me, don't you, Sarge, I always felt like you did. Why do you always make yourself out like a rock? One day I can come up and talk to you and the next day it's like we never even met." Welsh's relationship with Private Witt is never all that clear; he seems to treat Witt with a strange sense of brotherly love, and sometimes admiration: "You still believing in the beautiful light, are you? How do you do that? You're a magician to me," Welsh says to Witt in the roofless house.

Taken at face value, Welsh's dialogues with Witt suggest Welsh's yearning for something more than he already has. They seem to cause in him a need to "touch the glory," to see the light. Read from his materialist perspective, however, it all becomes nothing more than a series of cynical dialogues that attempt to mock Witt's way of living. From this perspective, the phrase "Where's your spark now?," the last line we hear Welsh say to Witt while standing by his grave (Figure 3), is not the opening remark to a possible soliloquy regarding the "spark" Witt claims to have seen in Welsh, but rather a dark and cynical statement that Witt's sensitivity to the "spark" did not exempt him from the perils of mortality.

Figure 3

We last see Welsh alive and well in a field, his body and non-world intact, reiterating once again that he has won, that the war has not destroyed his island. His world has not collapsed. Nothing has changed for Welsh from how things were at the beginning of Guadalcanal. He still holds that "everything you hear or see" remains a lie. They still "want you dead or in their lie" because "you are in a box, a moving box."

Spiritual immortality, or demise without dying

Private Witt's attentive wandering across the battlefield of Guadalcanal is a journey into the heart of spiritual immortality. We first hear Witt talk about "immortality" while he reminisce, amid the beauty of an earthly paradise, about his mother's death:

> I remember my mother when she was dying, she was all shrunk up and gray. I asked her if she was afraid, She shook her head no. I was afraid to touch the death I seen in her. I couldn't find nothing beautiful or uplifting about her going back to God. I wondered what it'd be like when I died, to know that this was the last breath you was ever going to draw. I just hoped I could meet it with the same calm she did. Cause that's where it's hidden. The immortality I hadn't seen.

There are two important issues that this soliloquy reveals. On the one hand, it tells us how, in being present at his mother's death, Witt was able for the very first time to come into contact with something beyond demise. His mother's death marks a point of departure in Witt's journey towards spiritual invulnerability. On the other hand, the soliloquy reveals to us where Witt believes this immortality resides. He sees it in his mother's eyes when she meets death with *calmness*. Others have misread the soliloquy by moving too swiftly to Heideggerian distinctions to make sense of it. The first misreading lies in arguing that the calmness Witt seeks is indistinguishable from or similar to Heidegger's notion of *anxiety*.[3] The second is to conclude that Witt is fascinated or concerned with demise, and thereby in becoming fearless in the face of it (see Silverman 2003).

Contending that calmness is identical with Heideggerian anxiety results from a misreading of the film—and of Heidegger, for that matter.

According to Heidegger, one is authentic in so far as one lives in constant anxiety (Heidegger 1962: 311), and that means accepting the ground-lessness of human existence while remaining steadfastly committed to one's defining commitment and yet open to the possible anomalies that threaten the collapse of one's current way of life. In other words, being-towards-death authentically implies that, if an individual's current "world" or identity collapses, the individual will accept the collapse and show steadfastness as well as flexibility by accepting the anomalies in his or her current experience as the basis of a new identity. Such authentic individuals are open to the possibility of "world collapse," and thereby the possibility of taking up a new identity and making a new beginning. This anxious authentic mode of existence differs totally from the sort of invulnerability to "world collapse" that Witt exhibits. Witt is invulnerable to world collapse because he is open to an indestructible world. What Witt comes to experience is spiritual immortality, not authentic death.

By being in touch with another world, Witt, as we will argue, like Welsh, is invulnerable to world collapse because, like Welsh, he doesn't have a world in Kierkegaard's and Heidegger's sense. He doesn't form defining commitments or expect to find meaning, and so does not live in a vulnerable world. Not only is the calmness in the face of demise Witt achieves categorically distinct from the anxiety of the authentic individual in the face of possible world collapse, but the spiritual illumination he achieves opens him to a world that can never collapse.[4]

Still, to claim that Witt has a fascination or concern with demise is not wholly unfounded. Throughout the film Witt comforts dying soldiers. He was afraid to touch his dying mother, but as he walks side by side with death in a lead-drenched battlefield he stares at a dying bird in wonder, and meets his own demise with absolute *calmness*. Witt's destiny seems to be somehow linked with the dying. After he has been AWOL in the Melanesian paradise, Welsh tells Witt how he is going to be punished: "I'm sending you to a disciplinary outfit. You'll be a stretcher-bearer. You'll be taking care of the wounded." Ultimately Witt is not sent to the disciplinary outfit to care for the wounded. Rather, when he is reintegrated into C-Company as they take on Hill 210, Witt decides to take on the duty of comforting the dying soldiers left behind. When, by a freak accident, Sergeant Keck blows off part of his lower body with a grenade and panics, the soldiers nearby are in a state of shock, yelling out empty promises. In contrast Witt holds him in his arms with absolute calmness: "You're gonna be alright. Even if you die. You didn't let your brother down," Witt says to Keck before he dies. Is the calmness Witt radiates the sort he saw in his dying mother's eyes? Is Witt no longer afraid of demise? By touching the dying soldier, does Witt show that he has attained spiritual immortality?

By touching "death," holding "death," and seeing "death," Witt is only soothing a dying world in his arms. He does not yet attain spiritual immortality. The calmness with which he handles the dying, however, does show us that he is no longer afraid to leave this world, to take the last breath he spoke of when remembering his mother's death. At this point of his journey Witt has already seen "another world," he has "touched the glory," and experienced "the shining." Witt's concern for the dying, and the courage he displays in the face of death, are symmetrically opposed to Welsh's cynical invulnerability: their invulnerability somehow draws them to each other and each of them to comfort the dying, the suffering, the vulnerable. At the world's end, the invulnerable comfort the vulnerable, or so Malick seems to believe.

A second feature that sheds light on the idea that Witt is not fixated on demise, but rather drawn to the frailty of those who are dying, is his selfless and courageous actions in battle. Not unlike Welsh, Witt's concern for comforting the vulnerable leads him to perform courageous actions on several occasions, actions that, although they are not patriotically heroic in essence but rather disconcerting and almost foolish, reveal a sacrificial and selfless attitude. Towards the end of the film, after the taking of Hill 210, Captain Band desperately looks for volunteers to "find out where the line is being cut" by the Japanese soldiers approaching the camp. Band orders Coombs and Fife to go. Witt, against all rational judgment, gladly volunteers to go with them. "I'll go," he says, "I want you to know I think the whole thing's a bad idea, though. If they come down here in any strength, Lieutenant, they'll knock our position to hell." Captain Band insists that Witt does not have to go, to which Witt replies that he wants to be there "in case something bad happens." Witt's sense of his invulnerability makes him prone to take courses of action that risk his life because nothing can endanger his world. But he does so only to help those who are more vulnerable than he is, those whose world can easily collapse in the light of demise.

At the beginning of the film, after Witt has been forced to return from the Melanesian paradise, Welsh refers to Witt as a punk recruit that has been AWOL more than once in six years of duty, a soldier who has not "learned a thing" in all his time in the army. As we have already claimed, at this point in Witt's journey, he has already come in contact with and attained a fragile form of invulnerability by having "seen another world," as he says to Welsh. So if Witt senses he is invulnerable, why does he flee the war and his duty as a soldier? Perhaps, the answer is that he doesn't *flee* at all, but rather is simply attracted by the shining he can see in the Melanesian paradise.

What allows us to say that Witt is in fact invulnerable upon his first encounter with Welsh on the ship, and that he is not merely imagining what he saw and experienced, is what we'll call Witt's early aesthetic understanding of immortality. When Witt first mentions to Welsh that he's "seen another world" after having been AWOL, Witt is referring both to the paradisiacal world where he swam with the Melanesian children as well as to his mother's *calmness* upon demise. In other words, the "world" Witt is referring to is the aesthetic sphere of immortality. To have an aesthetic understanding of immortality is to have a perspective on the world that selectively categorizes things by aesthetic values. Previous to Guadalcanal, Witt's aesthetic perspective draws him to things that radiate serenity and beauty, and repels him from things such as war, demise, and suffering. In Witt's aesthetic sphere of understanding, the "shining," the "glory," and the immortality that he "seeks" are manifest in all things whose beauty is self-evident, especially amidst a quasi-hedonistic distant paradise where humans live in harmony with nature, death, and one another. This is light years away from the nightmare of war. In other words, the reason why he abandons the war and his duty as a soldier is that he does not yet have a full understanding of where invulnerability is to be found.

"Does our ruin benefit the earth, aid the grass to grow, and the sun to shine? Is this darkness in you too? Have you passed through this night?" asks Witt after the taking of Hill 210. The battle of Guadalcanal, the night Witt passes through, marks the development of Witt's understanding of immortality from the aesthetic to the spiritual. By embracing the darkness of the world he sees beyond aesthetic invulnerability and begins to grasp spiritual invulnerability. By comforting the dying, by acting courageously, by seeing worlds vanish, Witt does not learn anything about demise. Instead, the threat of world collapse all around him allows him gradually to grasp what the spiritual immortality he's attained really is—what it allows him to see, to know, and to be. Once Witt has seen the encroaching darkness he questions whether his earlier experience of the pure shining of Melanesian life was an illusion. He realizes that what he took to be pure shining was, indeed, illusory. When he returns to the battlefield he begins to see the shining without denying the worlds collapsing all around him. He learns he has to accept darkness to see the brightness. The war has shed a new light upon a world that can never collapse because in that world things shine in a way he has never seen before.

The shining gradually dawns over the whole as Witt's attunement progresses from aesthetic to spiritual invulnerability. There is no moment of conversion in Witt's spiritual journey, no lightning bolt on the road to Damascus, but a series of experiences that slowly shed new light over his world. Witt goes from seeing the shining only in the Melanesian children and then seeing it threatened by darkness, to seeing the light even in "rocks" such as Welsh, in the midst of a collapsing world. After Witt has been exposed to the brutalities of war, Welsh asks him if he's "still believing in the beautiful light." Witt looks Welsh in the eyes, into the invulnerable stone who believes he is in a moving box and says to him, "I still see a spark in you."

A close-up of a bird, either being born or dying, appears after a heated battle (Figure 4), and Witt's voiceover emphasizes what distinguishes him from Welsh: "One man looks at a dying bird and thinks there's nothing but unanswered pain. That death's got the final word; it's laughing at him. Another man sees that same bird, feels the glory, feels

Figure 4

something smiling through it." The striking image of the bird allows us to see Witt's point in all clarity. Though the image is of a newly hatched bird, what we see looks so gruesome and stark that Witt's voiceover turns the image into both a bird in agony and a miracle of life. Thanks to Witt we see the bird from two perspectives, though never at the same time. We see the unanswered pain laughing at us as well as a shining without end smiling into our eyes. For Witt, at this stage of his spiritual journey the shining and the darkness of the world reside together in all things, including the Melanesians who struggle with disease and inner conflict, as Witt has seen in his second visit to their island. They, nonetheless, shine like a rosy-fingered dawn or a blue butterfly flying across a battlefield, brought out by their contrast with the darkness of demise and of the destruction of worlds.

On the threshold of demise, Witt, unlike any of us and, as far as we know, any of the soldiers that fought at Guadalcanal, has managed to see the glory at all times, in all places, in all things. At gunpoint, in a field, in a calmness that reminds us of his mother's, Witt meets his demise without ever dying as he joins the shining he has learned to experience. We hear his voice still, saying: "Oh, my soul. Let me be in you now. Look out through my eyes. Look out at the things you made. All things shining." Witt's immortal voice reaches out to us as the film ends. We see him swimming again with a group of sunbathed Melanesian children. Then, as we drift away from Guadalcanal, the last three images we see are of children in a boat, colorful birds on a tree, and a sprouting coconut growing in the sea, humans, animals, plants all shining.

Notes

1 For an example of an author who claims Malick mainly deals with mortality in *The Thin Red Line*, see Silverman 2003.
2 Compare, here, the description of the Knight of Infinite Resignation in Kierkegaard 1986: 72–3.
3 Simon Critchley also makes this point in his 2008.
4 To put this in Kierkegaardian terms, Witt is not a Knight of Faith in the sense of what Kierkegaard calls "Religiousness B," or paradoxical religiousness. (The distinction between "Religiousness A" and "Religiousness B" is drawn by Climacus in Kierkegaard 1941.) That highest form of human being according to Kierkegaard lucidly accepts the vulnerability of an unconditional commitment and yet has the "absurd" faith that he will never lose it. Rather,

Witt's existential stance resembles a non-Christian form of what Kierkegaard calls "Religiousness A." People with this sort of faith accept their life and world as a gift for which they feel gratitude and on the basis of which they feel secure. But Malick, like later Heidegger, plays down any sense of guilt, resignation, or latent anxiety which is essential to Kierkegaard's Christian account of Religiousness A, and instead emphasizes the glory and shining the pre-Socratic Greeks experienced as wonder in the face of the world.

References

Critchley, S. (2008) "Calm: on Terrence Malick's The Thin Red Line," in this volume, pp. 11–27.

Heidegger, M. (1962) Being and Time, trans. J. Macquarrie and E. Robinson, New York: Harper and Row.

Kierkegaard, S. (1986) Fear and Trembling, London: Penguin Books.

—— (1941) Concluding Unscientific Postscript, Princeton, NJ: Princeton University Press.

Lear, J. (2007) Ethics in the Face of Cultural Devastation, Cambridge, MA: Harvard University Press.

Silverman, K. (2003) "All Things Shining," in Loss, Berkeley, CA: University of California Press.

Chapter 4

David Davies

VISION, TOUCH, AND EMBODIMENT IN *THE THIN RED LINE*

Introduction: the problem of reading The Thin Red Line

IN THE OPENING SCENE OF Terrence Malick's visually stunning yet deeply enigmatic film *The Thin Red Line*, a crocodile inches its way into water covered with a green film of vegetation and slips beneath the surface (Figure 5). Against a backdrop of sunlight shafting through the high tops of trees, a voiceover asks, in a slow drawl: "What's this war in the heart of nature?" Ostensibly a war movie based on James Jones's novel of the same name about the battle for Guadalcanal, Malick's film has infuriated or enthralled viewers since its release. While those

Figure 5

who dismiss the film as a bad war movie have clearly misunderstood what they are watching, there is little consensus amongst those who are broadly favorable to the film as to what it is about, if not "war" in the conventional sense. A survey of the critical and philosophical literature reveals an astonishing diversity of readings, of which the following may serve as a representative sample.

Thomas Doherty (1999) reads the film as a post-Vietnam war movie, in the tradition of *Apocalypse Now* and *The Deer Hunter*, which explores the "darkness" in the American soul. This is perhaps the most straightforward kind of reading, but is difficult to reconcile with the narrative structure of the film, the role accorded to images of nature, and the overtly philosophical or religious dimension to the voiceovers that punctuate the narrative. Similar difficulties beset readings of the film as an attempt to undermine our generic expectations of the war movie in pursuit of a more "realistic" portrayal of the subject (see, for example, Flanagan 2003; McGettigan 2003).

These difficulties have led a number of critics to claim that the narrative operates at the level of myth rather than history. Ron Mottram (2003) interprets the film in broadly Christian terms, as an engagement with myths, central to the American consciousness, concerning a state of paradise lost, the possibility of redemption, and the origins of evil. At the core of Malick's cinema as a whole, and of *The Thin Red Line* in particular, is the expression of "an Edenic yearning to recapture a lost wholeness of being, an idyllic state of integration with the natural and the good both within and without ourselves" (2003: 14). In a similar voice, Robert Silberman speaks of Malick's "Edenic mythologizing" (2003: 165; see also Chion 2004: 8), while John Streamas, combining this theme with the first reading, characterizes the film as "a reinvented myth of the Fall filtered through a Vietnam-era political consciousness" (2003: 139).

Some find a different kind of transcendence in Malick's narrative, aligning him not with Christian mythology but with American Transcendentalism of the sort expounded by Emerson (Power 2003) and Thoreau (Mottram 2003). The idea here is that Nature and Soul are the elements making up the universe, and that the individual can attain a kind of unity with the world-soul through communing with nature. Those sympathetic to such a reading point to various themes that can be found in the voiceovers of Private Witt (Jim Caviezel)—talk of all men having "one big soul," as being part of "one self," of reaching out "to touch the glory," and, echoing Emerson, of "all things shinin'."[1] It is in these terms, it is claimed, that we can understand the "calm" and "immortality" of which Witt speaks in discussing his mother's death.

Others, however, find very different intellectual affinities in such talk, and in the film as a whole. Simon Critchley (this volume), while warning against any easy identification of a philosophical "message" in the film, argues that it should be seen as a meditation on mortality. The key idea, represented both in his words and in his actions by Witt, is that one should strive to face death, and the vicissitudes of life, with a certain "calm" akin to that comprised by the Heideggerian conception of *Angst* that attends Dasein's confrontation with its own being-towards-death. Hubert Dreyfus and Camilo Prince (this volume) also bring Heideggerian themes to bear on the film, appealing to a distinction between demise, as physical death, and ontological death, which involves a collapse of Dasein's world. It is the latter, and our ways of relating to it, rather than the former that is the real subject of the film, on this reading.

Finally, in a more full-bloodedly Heideggerian reading, Marc Furstenau and Leslie MacAvoy (2003) describe *The Thin Red Line* and Malick's other films as "Heideggerian cinema." Malick, they claim, is both expressing, in the content of his film, Heidegger's ontological critique of technology, and also realizing, in the working of the film on the audience, the role that Heidegger ascribes to the "poet in destitute times" by revealing, through the medium of cinema, the presencing of Being through language. Witt's voiceovers, they maintain, raise the question of Being in a philosophical manner. Robert Clewis (2003) also offers a Heideggerian reading of *The Thin Red Line*, taking its subject, again most clearly articulated through Witt, to be "ontic wonder."[2]

Associated with these readings of the thematic meaning of *The Thin Red Line* we find radically opposed interpretations of the many representations of nature in the film. For Critchley, Malick's cinema expresses a broadly naturalistic conception of nature. Nature, non-enchanted, is a warring force that frames the human drama of war but is utterly indifferent to human purposes and intentions. Human death is one more manifestation of the relentlessness of nature, in the face of which calmness is the only valid human response. In Mottram's reading of the film as "Edenic myth," on the other hand, nature is "a powerful sign of a higher good" (2003: 15): natural images of light, wind, trees, and skies "function as a bridge to another world and as a sign of its existence" (ibid.). Similarly, for the Transcendentalists, Malick presents nature as the spiritual realm, with which communion enables us to transcend the individual strivings expressed in war. Finally, for Silberman, the central theme of the film, manifested through the images of human and non-human nature, is the impenetrability of nature itself—is it cruel or kind, beautiful or ugly?—and the problem of human action in the face of this impenetrability: "It is in the visuals of the landscape . . . that Malick is able to most clearly express his vision of the world as paradise and paradise lost, caught up in darkness and death but open to redemption through the radiance of unselfish individual action" (2003: 171).

Of course, Malick's films are among the most celebrated examples of contemporary cinematic art, and it is to be expected that great works of art will support a plurality of interpretations. But the range and diversity of readings of *The Thin Red Line* surely calls for some explanation. A number of factors may help us to understand why this film has been read in such widely different ways:

(1)   First, four different kinds of contentful elements are interwoven in the experienced fabric of the film, every sequence containing at least two of these elements in some kind of juxtaposition. There is, first, a "war narrative" of a not completely unfamiliar type comprising a series of episodes in the battle for Guadalcanal. We follow the fates of individual soldiers, see the tensions between members of the military hierarchy and experience the camaraderie between members of the ranks. Moral dilemmas are posed and individuals act in morally assessable ways—some exhibit bravery or compassion, others cowardice or cruelty, and so on. While the film departs significantly from our generic expectations for the war movie (see "Introduction," this volume), it nonetheless contains an intelligible combat narrative that the viewer is expected to grasp, even if it isn't the thematic center of the film.

Second, as already noted, there are voiceovers (mainly in the voice of Witt) raising philosophical or theological questions about good and evil, the nature and origin of war in a number of senses, and how one should conduct oneself in the face of what life presents. Third, there are stunning visual representations of nature, especially shots of light filtered through high dense trees, water, long grass shaped by wind, the play of the sun on the landscape, and exotic fauna and flora. Rarely remarked, but also of considerable significance, are the acoustic representations of nature—the wind soughing through the long grass, the sounds of exotic birds and animals, the rushing water in the river through which the company is moving late in the film. Finally, there is a musical soundtrack replete with leitmotifs and culturally resonant elements—for example, quotations from Charles Ives' *The Unanswered Question* and the development, in Hans Zimmer's haunting score, of melodic ideas from the missionary song that features early in the diegesis and in the closing credits of the film. The viewer trying to grasp the film's thematic meanings must seek to establish how these elements interact. For example, does the narrative exemplify, or call into question, the ideas expressed in the voice-overs, or do these ideas contribute in some other way to the workings of the film? Do the representations of nature frame, or comment on, or expressively embellish, the narrative and interrogatory threads?

(2)   If we seek to throw light on these matters by recourse to the filmmaker's intentions as set out in the screenplay, we face further difficulties. The narrative of the film is adapted from James Jones's book of the same name, but Malick has changed the ending, the narrative focus, the attention to bodily violation and sexuality in war (see Power 2003), and the names and identities of many characters. Furthermore, Malick's second draft screenplay, which dates from fairly late in the making of the film, differs in many crucial respects from the final cut. In particular, the voiceovers, in which most of the apparent philosophical content of the film is contained, are neither in the novel nor in that screenplay, and were presumably added in post-production, when the film was cut down from around seven hours to close to three hours.[3]

(3)   It is tempting to see Malick's training as a philosopher as the key to unraveling the film. His undergraduate work with Cavell, his graduate work on Heidegger, and his translation of the latter's *Von Wesen des Grundes*, have suggested to some critics that it is in the writings of Heidegger that one can find the key to unlocking the obscurity of Malick's films.[4] Simon Critchley, however, while (as noted above), offering a reading that can be connected to Heideggerian themes, warns against reading the film as the expression of a philosophical pre- or metatext.

(4)   Finally, Malick is notoriously reluctant to discuss the thematic content (or indeed other aspects) of his films, thereby tacitly enfranchising

the sort of plurality of readings sketched above. We have, as interpretive resources, only a couple of interviews following the release of *Badlands*, some biographies of, or interviews with, cinematographers and actors who have worked with Malick, and a DVD—with no direct contribution by Malick—on the making of *The New World*. In the case of *The Thin Red Line*, the most informative source is an extended interview with John Toll, the cinematographer who worked with Malick on this film (Pizzello 1999). But Toll's acquaintance with the film stretches no further than the end of the shooting, and therefore does not illuminate the transformations that the film underwent in post-production which were responsible for the elements in the film that present the most difficult interpretive challenges.

Vision, touch, and embodiment in *The Thin Red Line*

My aim in this chapter is to point to something that I think has been either missed altogether or only partly grasped by the critical responses of which I am aware, and that may help us to fit these readings together and see what is right and what is wrong in each of them. I shall identify what I take to be a central theme in the film through which it not only engages (without answering) the philosophical questions posed in the dialogic and monologic content, but does so in a uniquely cinematic way, thereby exemplifying the philosophical possibilities of cinema. What commentators have missed or misunderstood is the centrality, in the cinematic presentation of the narrative and in some of the voiceovers, of the visual and the tactile, as inflections of our cognitive engagement with the world in which we act and are acted upon, and of the ways in which these inflections can be integrated with or divorced from one another. It is tempting, in fact, to distinguish two distinct modes of cognitive engagement—"visual" and "tactile"—that are associated in the film with conflict, struggle, cruelty, and instrumentalization, on the one hand, and with reconciliation, love, mercy, and understanding, on the other. But this would be a fatal oversimplification, since the film itself, both thematically and cinematically, overcomes this opposition and serves as a model of what might be termed "tactile vision," as a mode of embodied seeing and embodied agency.

Let me first identify a number of ways in which the visible and the tangible are thematized in *The Thin Red Line*, and then suggest how we might bring these threads together into some kind of coherent pattern.

(1)   One striking but generally overlooked feature of the film is the dehumanizing, distancing, objectifying, and instrumentalizing role some-times ascribed to vision. In the attack on Hill 210, Lt Col Tall (Nick Nolte), directing the slaughter of the men in Charlie company through binoculars, is charged by Capt. Staros (Elias Koteas), who is at the front, with failing to understand what is going on. The distanced visual (and technologically enhanced) (mis)apprehension of events by Tall is contrasted with the apprehension of those events by those who, like Staros, are caught up in the tactile, acoustic, olfactory, and visual sensory bombardment of battle, as conveyed by Malick's images.[5] Again, later in the film, as Witt and two of the company are sent ahead down a river to scout for the approaching enemy, the action is punctuated by shots of the eyes of an owl seeking its prey. And, in a metaphorical presentation of the same identification of (technologically enhanced) vision and instrumentalization, we are shown the Japanese machinegun post that is mowing down the American troops assaulting Hill 210 only through the "eyes" of the slit in the bunker on the hill.

(2)   Witt, on the other hand, is partly defined in the film by his tactile gestures, his reaching out to touch others. We see this initially in his interactions with the children in the village on the Melanesian island where the film opens, and in the flashback to his mother's death, where we presume that it is Witt's hand that is grasping hers (Figure 1). We see this later in his reaching out to touch the dying Sgt Keck (Woody Harrelson) and, after the taking of Hill 210, in his extending his hand to a terrified Japanese prisoner. The clearest example, however, occurs in an extended shot during the "leave" period after the assault on Hill 210, when we follow Witt through the camp where other members of the company are engaged in various forms of relaxation. He reaches out to touch and acknowledge each person he passes, and then the camera cuts away to a pair of clasped hands, presumably of one of the local guides. As the camera cuts back to Witt's face, his eyes clearly repre-sented as looking at the hands, we see tears forming in his eyes as he turns away. Finally, both in the opening sequences on the Melanesian island and in the shots that follow his death, we see him swimming underwater with the local boys, through the tactile resistance of the aqueous medium.

(3)   But also, as a number of critics have noted, the film suggests both through its dialogue and through its pictorial presentation of the narrative, that in some sense Witt differs from others in what he *sees*. The theme of Witt's seeing is announced very early in the film when, in his interview with Sgt Welsh (Sean Penn) after being returned to the ship after his period AWOL, he responds to Welsh's remark that "there ain't no world but this one" by insisting that he has "seen another world" (an insistence of which much is made by those offering Christian and Transcendentalist readings of the film). The theme is reiterated in a voiceover much later in the film when, to images of Welsh walking through the camp while the campfires are being extinguished, the voice-over (probably Witt, although there is some uncertainty about this) talks of how two men can see the same dying bird, yet, while one sees only pain and death, the other "sees the glory." Critchley (this volume) remarks, of this passage, that Welsh and Witt are presented as seeing different things in the same situation.

Furthermore, as a number of commentators not otherwise conspicuous for their concord have noted, the film often seems to be showing things "through Witt's eyes." Consider, for example, Martin Flanagan's comments on the way in which Malick presents the assault on Hill 210:

> Characteristic Malickian grace notes occur in the midst of the confusion, with shafts of light piercing through the long grass (such moments are usually relayed to a reverse shot of Witt, establishing the different register with which he seems to perceive events; although a peripheral figure in the action of the attack, Witt's viewpoint is frequently adopted.
>
> 2003: 134

Power makes a similar point, stating that Malick frames the images in the way Witt would see them—"quiet, calm, and untainted" (2003: 153). The most extended treatment of this idea, however, is to be found in Bersani and Dutoit's book *Forms of Being: Cinema, Aesthetics, Subjectivity*. They take the key to the film to be what they term "Witt's look," which "simply connects to the world through what might seem like a distancing from it: an evenness of witnessing" (2004: 158). This look, they maintain, "defines a cinematic aesthetic, and ethic, of implicated witnessing, of a witnessing identical to total absorption" (2004: 161).

I want to suggest that we should see the first of these "attributes" of Witt—his relating to the human and non-human world through touch, broadly construed—as the key to understanding the second—the distinctive nature of Witt's "look" and the sense to be made of the idea that he "sees another world." Bersani and Dutoit are right, I think, to resist the Transcendentalist reading of such talk of another world: they argue that the "other world" is "this world seen as a vast reservoir of correspondences" (2004: 169). They are wrong, however, to identify Witt's look as one of "ontological passivity," the look of "a subject divested of subjectivity" (2004: 164–5). Rather, the key to Witt's "seeing differently" lies in the way in which his seeing is integrated with his embodied engagement with his world. It is because Witt's seeing of the world is so fully integrated into his embodied engagement with things that he quite literally "sees another world," and his actions—the "calm" of which a number of critics speak—are the direct consequence of the world he sees. Witt's seeing of things as sensible and sentient surfaces, his, in this sense, "seeing feelingly" in the words of the blinded Gloucester in King Lear, is to be contrasted with the disembodied and instrumentalizing vision of Tall.

There is much more that needs to be said if we are to motivate this claim about the centrality of Witt's mode of tactile seeing to the thematic meaning of the film. In particular, one needs to correctly apprehend the significance and place in the film of Welsh's haunting final voiceover, as we see the emotionally and spiritually ravaged faces of the remaining members of Charlie company making their way to the troop ships for disembarkation. After reiterating his earlier observations about the "property" based nature of the war and rehearsing his personal credo for surviving in such circumstances—that the only thing a man can do is to find something that's his and turn himself into an island—his final words in the film are as follows: "If I never meet you in this world, let me feel the lack. One look from your eyes and my life will be yours." Surprisingly, most commentators who have considered this remark have taken it to indicate that Welsh has been converted to Witt's way of seeing things, and has recognized the need to be open to others. Bersani and Dutoit, for example, interpret these words as an expression, by Welsh, of "a yearning for something he lacks but to which he would give his life." Clewis also endorses such a reading, taking it to be a key piece of evidence for his claim that, by the end of the film, Welsh has undergone a profound transformation due to the influence of Witt, a transformation which, for Clewis, is "one of the most existentially significant elements" in the film (Clewis 2003: 34).

But this reading of Welsh's closing words makes no sense in light of the remarks that immediately precede them. The "lack" that Welsh wishes to feel is not the painful absence of others with whom he wishes to be in community, but the welcome absence of the demands of others that will imperil his defensive strategy. It is because, as is apparent in his relationship to Witt and his confession to not yet feeling "numb," he recognizes that the looks of others make demands upon him that he cannot resist. As Bersani and Dutoit rightly point out, the "look" of others, the way they are visually engaged by the worlds they see, is the way in which they present themselves to us, as embodied experiencers of the world to whose self-presentations we respond through our own embodied existence.

This brings me to another crucial feature of the film, and of Malick's cinema more generally, that has, I think, been misinterpreted by commentators. It is often remarked that Malick's films prescind from what is normally a central concern for narrative cinema, namely, the presentation of characters who are psychologically "thick" in that the motivations for their actions are made clear, usually through the dialogue in the diegesis. Indeed, if we compare Malick's films with their screenplays, it is clear that much of the motivational detail contained in dialogue in the screenplay has been deliberately excised from the film, so that the visual takes over from the verbal, and that this excision was in accordance with Malick's explicit instructions to the actors (see Morrison and Schur 2003: chapter 4, for details of this). Some of Malick's critics have even suggested that this is the reason why the voiceovers are needed, to make up for the unintelligibility of the film in the absence of some alternative way of communicating the psychological states of the characters.

But this line of thought takes as given a particular model of human action and of its intelligibility to others, where the latter requires that actions be seen as issuing forth from rational deliberation that can be represented as instrumental reasoning involving the beliefs and goals of the agent. On this widely accepted model in cognitive science, our capacity to make sense of the actions of others requires either the application of a "theory of mind" that traffics in such intentional ascriptions or the running, in a mental "simulator," of the intentional profile attributed to the other. Malick's characters, however, seem to respond to one another and to the world they encounter in a less deliberatively mediated way. They respond to the world that they see, as embodied agents, and perceive the actions of others as expressions of their human projects. They experience the world as calling on them to act in certain ways, and they respond to this call without prior reasoning of the sort required by the "instrumental model." Where action is represented as the result of instrumental deliberation, as in the case of Tall, it is seen as disconnected from what is actually going on. This manner of construing both our perception of others as "minded" and of the world as intentionally inflected relative to our purposes and embodied nature was elaborated philosophically by Merleau-Ponty (1962) and psychologically, in terms of "affordances," by J.J. Gibson (1979), and has recently been defended on the basis of contemporary work in the cognitive sciences by Shaun Gallagher (2005: especially chapters 1 and 9).

It is in terms of this model of human agency that we can understand Welsh's "courageous" action in running onto the field of battle to administer morphine to the screaming Tella: an action viewed by many commentators as mysterious given Welsh's professed philosophy—to look out only for oneself—and his admonition to Witt not to think that he can make any difference by sacrificing himself. Welsh responds to what the situation demands of him not as a result of any kind of moral reasoning, but because the world as he experiences it calls for such action. This also explains his violent response—that "it's all about property"— when Staros says he will recommend Welsh for a medal, something that categorizes his action as instrumentally courageous rather than as a human act called for and performed in response to Tella's suffering. Again, the contrast with Tall's inability to see his soldiers' need for water after the taking of Hill 210, and his instrumental reasoning about how best to take advantage of the situation, is striking.

If the characters in Malick's film are in general represented as acting in response to the demands that are made upon them by their embodied engagements with the world and with other embodied agents, what is distinctive of Witt, as noted above, is the nature of those engagements. All characters respond to the demands of the world that experientially presents itself to them—the world they "see"—but Witt sees a "different world" and thus experiences different demands in a given "objective" situation. For example, he sees the fear in the faces of Fife and Coombs when they are commanded to reconnoitre ahead to locate the enemy, and he immediately responds to this by volunteering to go with them, as something the situation demands of him. In this respect, Witt's embodied engagement with the world prefigures Malick's portrayal of the Powatin in *The New World*. Consider the instructions given to the "core group" of actors by the choreographer Raoul Trujillo: what Malick wants more than anything else, Trujillo says, is that "in the canoes, walking through the woods, whatever else, what separates you guys from the English is that you people are in complete harmony with the earth and the universe and everything that exists." It is through "the body language of the Indian people" that their story is to be told.[6]

The cinematic representation of embodied agency in *The Thin Red Line*

What I want to explore in the final section of this chapter is something that I think is crucial if we are to grasp the distinctive artistic qualities of Malick's film—the manner in which Malick communicates cinematically the quality of Witt's seeing, and of embodied cognition and agency in general, through the manner in which the narrative is visually represented. This is significant because it reveals how the film uses the cinematic medium in a distinctively philosophical way, and also addresses what might seem to be a central paradox in a film which in some respects seems to identify vision with objectification. One of the most striking features of the film for the viewer is the way in which Malick conveys the tactile and visceral qualities of the situations in which the action unfolds[7]—for example, in the brig of the ship before the landing on Guadalcanal, in the assault on the slopes of Hill 210, and in the mud of the captured Japanese village. Furthermore, while the soundtrack also plays an important part in this, the tactile and visceral qualities of the represented situations are for the most part given to us visually, by qualities of the images through which those situations are represented.

And, it is worth noting, it is not merely, as with Malick's other films, the visual beauty of the images, but their ability to convey touch, sensation, and visceral feeling that is striking.

How is this achieved? What Malick demonstrates, I think, is that the camera, like the eye, can objectify, distance, and dehumanize, but it can also convey things through their sensible qualities, and also, in so doing, convey the sensibilities of the characters portrayed. We have a model for this in the idea of a "painterly" style of representation that Wölfflin (1950) associates with Baroque art. "Painterly" differ from "linear" modes of representation in (a) the way in which form is articulated (through interplay between masses rather than outlines of masses); (b) the qualities of things through which they are represented (texture rather than shape); (c) the manner in which relationships between objects are conveyed (holistically rather than atomistically); and (d) the faculties through which pictorial articulation is primarily grasped (sensation rather than understanding).

Painterliness, so conceived, seems to be a quality of Malick's images also—they have a tactile, holistic quality, the camera representing things in terms of their textures, and acting as a medium that conveys things through their tangible as much as through their visible characteristics. This is achieved in a number of ways. First, and most obviously, the tactile qualities of things are conveyed through representations of touchings, as, most clearly, in the scenes of Private Bell (Ben Chaplin) and his wife, and of Witt as described above. Second, and more interestingly, things are represented in ways that accentuate their responsiveness to touch and pressure, as with the billowing curtains shown in the scenes of Bell and his wife, and the images of the grasses fanned by the wind during the assault on Hill 210. But, most significantly, the camera itself is presented as an embodied cognizer of the world. During Bell's reconnaissance of the bunker on Hill 210 and the later attack that he leads, the camera moves at the level of the advancing troops, pushing back the grasses. The same applies to the early advances of Charlie company after they disembark from the troop ships. The camera moves through its "environment" in a manner that recalls the opening scene as the alligator edges its way slowly into the murky water.[8]

But there is something else that is crucial to Malick's cinematic representation of human embodied consciousness, which serves to differentiate the latter from the feral embodiment of the alligator. Malick's painterly mode of depiction essentially involves the interplay between the elements identified earlier—the cinematic presentation of the narrative, the voiceovers, the depictions of nature, and the soundtrack. The use of music and of the soundtrack in general helps to communicate to us the *sense* of what is happening through our emotions and our sensibilities rather than through our intellects, it might be claimed. But what is the function of the voiceovers in the film?

The voiceovers were, with very few exceptions, added in post-production. They are one of two devices that stand in some kind of thematic relation to the visual narrative. The other device is the flashback, which is used to represent earlier episodes in the lives of specific characters. While it is always obvious which character's experiences are represented in the flashbacks, it is only sometimes easily determined to which character, if indeed any, the voiceovers are attributable. Where the source of the voiceover is clear, this is because of the voice itself, or the associated images, or the camera's dwelling on the character in question in a confirmatory way. In such cases, the function of the voiceover is also relatively clear—to represent the subjectivity of the character, thereby serving to provide psychological "thickness" that would otherwise be lacking. Bell's voiceovers combine with flashbacks to represent his very sensuous relationship with his wife. Tall's voiceovers represent his professional disenchantment, and Welsh's his personal view of the war—as all about "property"—and of how one can survive it—by making oneself a "rock."

But many of the other voiceovers play a more ambiguous role, starting with the opening line of the film: "What's this war in the heart of nature?" This is usually attributed to Witt, as are most of the other voiceovers that do not obviously play the "character-thickening" roles just noted. But some voiceovers are difficult to attribute because the cues that serve us well in other cases lead here to conflicting attributions. For example, the thematically significant voiceover comparing two ways in which we might see a dying bird seems to belong to Witt, given its content, but is visually accompanied by shots of Welsh walking through the camp dousing fires and is delivered in a voice that doesn't seem to match any of the other voiceovers. Some critics have nonetheless attempted attributions based on the traditional idea that the voiceover belongs to the character we are (mostly) looking at, leading to some bizarre attributions that make no sense given the rest of the movie (see, for example, Clewis 2003). Others have inferred that these voiceovers are not attributable to any particular character. It seems clear, however, that at least the majority of them are attributable to Witt. We may term these voiceovers, which are almost entirely interrogative in form and ask fundamental questions about the nature of evil and its presence in the world, "Witt voiceovers."

What is the function of the Witt voiceovers? Are they ways of "thickening" Witt as a character by showing that, behind the calm "folksy" exterior and demeanor, there is a stream of deep philosophical questioning? If so, it is strange that the role of philosophical questioning should be given to Witt rather than to Staros (Bersani and Dutoit 2004). Also, they seem to relate to the visually presented narrative differently from the character-thickening voiceovers, which are closely tied either to particular events in the narrative, or to flashbacks. The Witt voiceovers are only loosely diegetically anchored, and can occur when Witt is not present (the opening monologue) or is dead (the closing monologue).

If, in spite of these anomalies, we take the Witt voiceovers to be insights into his consciousness during the battle, we may be sympathetic to the Heideggerian reading of the film according to which Witt is engaged in the primary philosophical activity of raising the question of Being. Alternatively, we may simply ascribe to all of the voiceovers the single function of contributing "to the construction of character, synthesizing impersonal chronicle with stream-of-consciousness poetics" (Morrison and Schur 2003: 26; Clewis 2003: 22, 29). Others, however, are more sceptical, maintaining that the Witt voiceovers "are crucial to the film's sense, but they have very little intellectual weight" (Bersani and Dutoit 2004: 132). Their function then is to provide a background of linguistically mediated questioning to which no linguistic answer is either provided or available: it is in the visual presentation of Witt's way of visually engaging with the world that the answer to these questions lies.

Bersani and Dutoit are right, I think, in concluding that the Witt voiceovers cannot be taken to express morals illustrated by the narrative, for they function mainly in the interrogative mode, asking questions that are in no clear sense answered by what is depicted. Furthermore, the cinematically presented narrative undermines the "commentary" in a number of ways—most obviously when Witt's assertion "war doesn't enoble men, it turns them into dogs" is undercut by some of the actions performed, by the unbearable shame felt afterwards by those who are temporarily turned into "dogs," and, as Critchley (this volume) and Furstenau and MacAvoy (2003) both note, by the tendency of war, as an extreme situation, to reawaken in participants a sense of their mortality and thereby of their humanity.

What unifies Malick's different uses of the voiceover device in *The Thin Red Line* is that the voiceovers present the viewer with a stream of reflective thinking that generally stands apart from the actions of the characters. The voiceovers serve, along with the depictions of nature, as the frame for the human actions presented—actions that are always those of embodied agents whose embodied actions are permeated by language and conceptual awareness. Consider, here, Bell's recollections of his wife evoked by the clinging of the grass to his body as he squirms up to survey the machinegun post prior to the taking of Hill 210 (Figure 6). As embodied consciousnesses, the world "touches us" not merely physically but emotionally, and awakens in us memories that permeate our awareness of the world, even (or perhaps especially) in those moments where our animal nature is most at risk. But the reflections expressed in the voiceovers do not standardly motivate the actions of the characters, although they represent, in many cases, the way in which the characters conceptualize their engagements with the world. As argued above,

Figure 6

action, in Malick's films, while motivated, is not generally presented as intelligible in terms of the sorts of psychological deliberations familiar from intentional psychology. It is intelligible as agency called forth by the experiences of embodied agents, although it can obviously be reconstructed in intentional terms. But, if the thought processes presented discursively in the voiceovers and visually, as memories, in the flashbacks do not usually function to provide us with insights into motivation, they do identify how human embodied agency differs from the embodied agency of the crocodile seen slipping beneath the surface of the water in the opening shot of the film. In this way, the two devices play an essential part in Malick's cinematic presentation of the manner in which the human agent encounters and responds to its world.

I think this helps to explain why the effect on the viewer of a film like The Thin Red Line in no way decreases on repeated viewings. The film engages us not through involving us in the narrative in any standard way, but by expressing, and making us aware of, the richness and complexity of our embodied engagement with the world. It also makes us aware (perhaps) of the war in the heart of our own nature, the perilous balance between our primitive embodied agency in the world, represented most sharply by those moments in the height of the battle when there is only time to respond to immediate sensory stimulation, and our equally inhuman rationality, represented by Tall who cogitates his way through the film, always weighing what he has lost and what he has gained, always looking over his shoulder, as when Staros defies him.[9]

It is important to clarify one final aspect of Malick's treatment of his themes. As noted by Power (2003: 149ff.), Malick, in adapting Jones's novel, "excises" the body by removing the graphic depictions of physical carnage and sexual arousal that are central to Jones's representation of the experience of battle: "The body is simply not as much of a concern for Malick." But this failure to dwell on the experience of the body is quite consistent with the thematization of embodied perception and agency that I have stressed, since the latter relates to the way in which a world is given to us through embodiment, and is essentially shaped by that embodiment.

At the thematic centre of The Thin Red Line, then, are the possibilities implicit in our perceptual engagement with the natural and human world, from which vision can distance us in an instrumentalizing fashion or with which vision can connect us, as self-consciously embodied perceivers and agents. It is the latter mode of visual engagement that Witt represents, and his actions differ from those of others around him not because he responds to the world he sees but because of the embodied nature of the way he sees the world. This, finally, allows us to understand what "the thin red line" is for Malick. It is not, as it was for Jones, the line between sanity and madness. Rather, it is the skin, signifying our embodiment as knowers. The central contrast, then, is not between vision and touch but between two forms of embodied cognition: one which objectifies what it cognizes, and one which reaches out to what it cognizes across "the thin red line."[10]

Notes

1 For Emerson, the soul is identical to the whole of nature, of which the sun, the moon, animals, and plants are all "shining parts." See Power 2003: 154.

2 Many of the interpretations of The Thin Red Line in Morrison and Schur (2003) are also anchored in a Heideggerian reading of Malick.

3 See Silberman 2003, and Morrison and Schur 2003: chapter 4, for this.

4 "Given that his first career was as a philosopher, the clues to Malick's films are readily available, and the supposed obscurities of his films may be illuminated by placing them within a specific philosophical tradition" (Furstenau and MacAvoy 2003: 174).

5 Martin Flanagan comments on the cinematic representation of the assault on Hill 210 that, in spite of the often-remarked "poetry" of Malick's images, it "combines sound and image in a way that is arguably more visceral than poetic" (2003: 134).

6 These quotations are taken from the film on "The making of The New World," included with the DVD of the film.

7 For a more detailed and very insightful examination of the cinematic devices that enable Malick to convey such things in The Thin Red Line, see Amy Coplan's chapter, this volume.

8 See, again, Amy Coplan's chapter, this volume, for insight into the technical means whereby these images were generated.

9 This reflex gesture by Tall is a subtle visual reference to Brigadier-General Quintard's (John Travolta) remark to Tall on the bridge of the boat prior to the landing on Guadalcanal: "there's always someone watching, like a hawk . . . always someone ready to jump in if you're not."

10 An earlier version of this chapter was presented at a panel on The Thin Red Line at the 2007 meetings of the Pacific Division of the American Society for

Aesthetics. I am grateful to all who offered feedback at that time, and, in particular, to my fellow panelists Amy Copland and Iain Macdonald. I also gratefully acknowledge the support of the Social Sciences and Humanities Research Council of Canada, a research grant from whom facilitated work on this chapter.

References

Bersani, L., and U. Dutoit (2004) *Forms of Being: Cinema, Aesthetics, Subjectivity*, London: British Film Institute Publishing.

Chion, M. (2004) *The Thin Red Line*, London: British Film Institute Publishing.

Clewis, R. (2003) "Heideggerean wonder in Terrence Malick's *The Thin Red Line*," *Film and Philosophy*, 7: 22–36.

Coplan, A. (2008) "Form and feeling in Terrence Malick's *The Thin Red Line*," this volume, 65–86.

Critchley, S. (2002) "Calm—on Terrence Malick's *The Thin Red Line*," *Film-Philosophy*, Vol. 6, No. 38. (http://www.film-philosophy.com/vol6-2002/n48critchley). A modifed version of this piece appears in this volume, 11–27.

Doherty, T. (1999) "Review of *The Thin Red Line*," *Cineaste* 24: 2–3.

Dreyfus, H. and C. Prince (2008) "*The Thin Red Line*: dying without demise, demise without dying," in this volume, 29–43.

Flanagan, M. (2003) "'Everything a Lie': the critical and commercial reception of Terrence Malick's *The Thin Red Line*," in Patterson, ed., 123–36.

Furstenau, M. and L. MacAvoy (2003) "Terrence Malick's Heideggerian cinema: war and the question of Being in *The Thin Red Line*," in Patterson, ed., 173–85.

Gallagher, S. (2005) *How the Body Shapes the Mind*, Oxford: Oxford University Press.

Gibson, J.J. (1979) *The Ecological Approach to Visual Perception*, Boston, MA: Houghton-Mifflin.

McGettigan, J. (2003) "*Days of Heaven* and the myth of the West," in Patterson, ed., 50–60.

Merleau-Ponty, M. (1962) *The Phenomenology of Perception*, trans. C. Smith, London: Routledge and Kegan Paul.

Morrison, J. and T. Schur (2003) *The Films of Terrence Malick*, London: Praeger.

Mottram, R. (2003) "All things shining: the struggle of wholeness, redemption, and transcendence in the films of Terrence Malick," in Patterson, ed., pp. 13–23.

Patterson, H. (ed.) (2003) *The Cinema of Terrence Malick: Poetic Visions of America*, London: Wallflower Press.

Pizzello, S. (1999) "The war within" (an interview with John Toll), *American Cinematographer*, 80: 2.

Power, S.P. (2003) "The other world of war: Terrence Malick's adaptation of *The Thin Red Line*," in Patterson, ed., 148–59.

Silberman, R. (2003) "Terrence Malick, landscape, and 'this war at the heart of nature'," in Patterson, ed., 160–72.

Streamas, J. (2003) "The greatest generation steps over the thin red line," in Patterson, ed., 137–47.

Wölfflin, H. (1950) *Principles of Art History*, New York: Dover.

Chapter 5

Amy Coplan

FORM AND FEELING IN TERRENCE MALICK'S *THE THIN RED LINE*

Introduction

TERRENCE MALICK'S 1998 FILM *The Thin Red Line* is a moving and complex film that "shows" far more than it "tells," and that appeals to the senses and the body at least as much as to the mind. Malick's highly distinctive cinematic style utilizes the resources of the film medium to create images and sounds that express and elicit feelings and associations in a way no other artistic medium or form of communication could. Very often his presentation of these images and sounds leaves them uninterpreted. Malick seems to trust viewers and thus, unlike the majority of Hollywood filmmakers, he rarely directs viewers on what to think or how to make sense of the sensory information on display. Because of this, *The Thin Red Line* has inspired numerous interpretations and evaluations, many of which have little in common.[1]

The main thing that distinguishes film from other art forms is its ability to create stories through the selective presentation of visual and aural information. This is especially true of Malick's films, which are more cinematic than most because they foreground features of experience that can only be communicated through appeal to the senses. In this essay, I will examine how Malick uses film form to express and elicit feeling. I do not offer this examination as an interpretation of the film but rather as a kind of prolegomenon or introduction to an interpretation. Why? Because before we begin theorizing at a high level about philosophical themes, meanings, and messages in a film, we must get clearer about the film's form and how it influences viewers' attention, perception, and feelings.

My primary purpose will be to illuminate the relationship between formal features of *The Thin Red Line* and the emotional, affective, and perceptual experiences the film evokes. Compared to standard Hollywood films, the cinematic style of the film is highly unconventional. One overall effect of this is that much of viewers' affective experience of the film is non-cognitive or minimally cognitive. Another is that viewers' perception and attention are often focused on sensory information. I will examine the film's unconventional style through an analysis of various filmmaking techniques that Malick and the other filmmakers used to construct an episodic narrative and to create numerous shots, scenes, and sequences that are highly subjective and impressionistic. These three formal features of the film—a highly subjective perspective, impressionistic images and sounds, and an episodic narrative—both distinguish the film from traditional Hollywood films and result in viewers having an overall emotional or affective experience of the film that is, at least initially, primarily perceptual and embodied rather than cognitive and evaluative.

While my analysis is not an attempt to interpret the deeper philosophical meaning or significance of the film's form, it should help to clear the way for such interpretations by explaining how Malick's formal choices lead to a distinctive type of spectatorial response. It begins at a lower level of explanation than most philosophy of film and film criticism in that its focus is on developing a descriptive account of how the film works rather than on an interpretation or evaluation of the film's meaning. At a more general level this analysis will help to show how particular aesthetic characteristics are created during the process of filmmaking and how cinematic techniques through cinematic style influence audience response.

Philosophers interested in film don't generally concern themselves with the technical aspects of filmmaking but instead tend to concentrate either on abstract or metalevel questions about issues such as the nature of film as an artistic medium or on uncovering the philosophical questions or themes in a specific film. And yet when it comes to films that seem philosophically interesting, philosophers' readings of the themes and meanings of a given film's content are usually based on interpretations of the film's form. Any account of the nature of film or of why a particular film should be read as communicating certain ideas requires at least some understanding of the mechanisms of cinematic style and of why particular formal choices arouse particular feelings and experiences in the viewer.

Cognitive emotions and non-cognitive affects

I argue that much of viewers' emotional or affective experience of *The Thin Red Line* is non-cognitive or minimally cognitive, but what does this mean and how do non-cognitive or minimally cognitive emotions or affects really differ from those that are cognitive? To answer these questions we need to know something about what emotion and affect are.

According to the cognitive theory of emotion, the dominant view in philosophy and psychology, prototypical emotions such as anger, fear, and disgust are mental states that either require or are identical to a cognitive evaluation or judgment and are directed at specific objects. Philosopher Robert Solomon describes emotions as evaluative judgments that structure our world (Solomon 2004) while philosopher Martha Nussbaum defines them as judgments assenting to value-laden appearances (Nussbaum 2004). For cognitive theorists, sadness either is or requires the belief or judgment that one has lost something valuable, and fear is or requires the belief or judgment that one's loved ones or oneself is in danger. Proponents of the cognitive theory of emotion don't deny that most emotions involve bodily feelings. Nevertheless, their accounts emphasize the cognitive dimensions of emotion.

Philosophers Jenefer Robinson and Jesse Prinz have challenged the cognitive theory of emotion and each has developed an alternative view informed by empirical research. Robinson characterizes emotions as ongoing causal processes that involve instinctive appraisals and cognitive reappraisals and ready us for appropriate action (Robinson 2005). Prinz argues that emotions are embodied appraisals, a special form of perception of the body and of our relations to the world (Prinz 2004). Robinson and Prinz accept that many emotion episodes involve cognition or are caused in part by a cognitive stimulus, but neither considers a cognitive judgment to be necessary for emotion since it is possible for us to respond emotionally to a perceptual stimulus in an immediate and automatic way prior to making a cognitive evaluation. Philosophers and psychologists often use the following sort of example to illustrate. Suppose I am walking in the woods and I see a curvy stick-shaped object on the ground. The mere visual perception of this object can be enough to make me afraid, and my fear can occur prior to my judging the object to be a snake or judging that the object is dangerous. I can go on to make such judgments but my fear response will be triggered first (LeDoux 1998).

Recent empirical evidence favors the type of theory held by Robinson and Prinz over the cognitive theory of emotion, and thus there is good reason to believe that emotions can be non-cognitive though they don't have to be. Nevertheless, even if one subscribes to a cognitive theory of emotion and thus denies the possibility of non-cognitive emotions, one can still acknowledge the existence of non-cognitive affect, a mental state closely related to emotion. Affect is a broad category that includes a wide range of mental states, all involving feelings and some type of physiological arousal. Affective states are not necessarily directed at specific objects nor do they necessarily involve cognitive evaluations or appraisals so even if there can be no non-cognitive emotions, there can be non-cognitive affective experiences including emotional contagion, moods, and automatic affective reflexes.

Emotional contagion is "the tendency to automatically mimic and synchronize expressions, vocalizations, postures, and movements with those of another person, and, consequently, to converge emotionally" (Hatfield *et al.* 1992: 153–4). In other words, emotion is transmitted from one person to another person; it is as though one individual "catches" the emotion of another. The main processes involved in contagion are motor mimicry and the activation and feedback from mimicry. Emotional contagion usually occurs so quickly that it is difficult to be fully aware of it as it is happening. I characterize it as a non-cognitive affective response because it occurs not as a result of a cognitive judgment or evaluation but automatically and involuntarily in response to the mere perception of others' emotions (Hatfield *et al.* 1992).

Another type of affective response that need not be cognitive is mood. Moods are affective states much like emotions but lacking highly specific objects and typically lasting for a longer duration than prototypical emotions. They include states such as free-floating anxiety, dread, depression, melancholy, gloom, and cheer. Psychologists and philosophers characterize moods as more globally oriented than emotions and as more diffuse. Moods can have nothing as their objects or everything as their objects. Moreover, moods often cannot be justified in the same way that emotions can because they lack specific objects. In spite of the differences between emotions and moods, they are very similar phenomenologically and we often use the same words to describe them.[2]

Automatic affective responses such as startle make up a third group of non-cognitive affective responses. These responses are universal and involuntary; they occur in response to sensory stimuli such as loud noises or sudden movements. Startle involves a characteristic facial expression, an immediate closing of the eyes, a widening of the mouth, an immediate galvanic skin response, and cardiac changes (that is, an increase in blood pressure and changes in breathing patterns) (Robinson 1995).

Form and feeling in *The Thin Red Line*

One of the distinguishing features of film as an artistic medium is its ability to produce non-cognitive affective responses, which viewers experience as a result of film's direct sensory engagement. Through the deployment of visual and aural information, film can evoke intense feelings in us that are independent of, and sometimes even incompatible with, our cognitive judgments of what we are watching (Smith 1995; Coplan 2006). This is part of what makes film such a powerful medium. Noël Carroll argues that through the use of various cinematic techniques, filmmakers are able to exploit these responses: "Manipulating such variables as speed, scale, lighting, and sound, among others, the filmmaker often appears to have direct access to our nervous system, bypassing the cerebral cortex and triggering automatic affective reflexes" (Carroll 2003: 524).

Elsewhere I have hypothesized that non-cognitive affective experiences occur in response to film far more often than we realize and that they play a more significant role in spectatorial response than the academic literature suggests (Coplan 2006). This happens even more often in Malick's films than in most because his cinematic style often discourages viewers from making the kinds of cognitive evaluations associated with cognitive emotions. The formal style of traditional Hollywood films, on the other hand, often aims to produce prototypical cognitive emotions with their clear intentionality and evaluative judgments.

Why does Malick's style evoke so many non-cognitive affects and how does he create that style? The answers to these questions will help to reveal the relationship between film form and audience response and will show how Malick's formal style takes advantage of the film medium and in so doing is more cinematic than the style of traditional Hollywood films. This is because Malick's films do more to directly engage the senses and maintain sensory and perceptual engagement and also elicit more non-cognitive affects than traditional films. Both direct sensory engagement and non-cognitive affects result from the specific ways in which films present information, which is why they rarely occur in response to literature.

As I've been arguing, compared to traditional Hollywood film, the cinematic style of *The Thin Red Line* is unconventional, especially for a war film with a big budget and several famous actors.[3] Although some scenes fit the standard model of narrative filmmaking, Malick uses a far less familiar cinematic rubric for the majority of the film. The story of what happens to the soldiers in C-Company after being brought to Guadalcanal is complicated and sometimes confusing. Rather than a straightforward plot with exposition, conflict, and resolution, we get a series of discrete, vivid moments, the meaning of which is rarely entirely clear. To put this in aesthetic terms, the narrative of the film is largely episodic. Malick does not seem especially concerned to present the story as a series of causes and effects that tell viewers precisely how everything they see and hear is related, which is what standard film narratives do.

Typically, stories are told in film through what Noël Carroll describes as "erotetic narration" (Carroll 2008). Structured by a clear beginning, middle, and end, the plots of these films unfold according to a model of questions and answers. At the beginning of the film, a question or series of questions is raised, and then the film goes on to answer the question, generating and answering new questions along the way. These questions organize the events and actions and provide the framework through which we interpret characters' thoughts, feelings, and intentions. Erotetic narration gives films a causal structure that specifies the relations among shots, scenes, sequences, and the various elements within them. This type of narration is so common that when a film isn't told in this way, it is often characterized as non-narrative.

Erotetic narration is the norm for Hollywood films in part due to its being highly effective at producing emotional responses through a process of criterial prefocusing. Criterial prefocusing is Noël Carroll's term for the process by which filmmakers foreground certain events and actions in the presentation of a narrative so that audience members will recognize them as fitting into familiar schemas that are likely to elicit an emotional reaction. Carroll accepts a version of the judgment theory of emotion for standard emotions, though he appreciates that it cannot explain the full range of filmgoers' affective experience (Carroll 2003: 523). Recall that on this view, emotion requires a judgment or belief, which is constitutive of or identical to emotion. For example, if I believe that X has wronged me or mine, then I feel anger toward X. The relevant judgment in this case is that X wronged me or mine, which corresponds to the emotion anger. Filmmakers attempt to ensure that viewers will respond emotionally by highlighting or focusing on actions, events, and character traits that fit the standard criteria for specific emotions. This process, which predisposes us to respond emotionally, is generally achieved through erotetic narration.[4]

Episodic narratives, by contrast, do not always make clear how various events, actions, and characters are related. Although there are still loose connections among various images and scenes, plots are rarely organized in terms of an underlying causal structure. As a result, episodic narratives are often characterized as non-narrative. Questions may still be raised but they aren't always answered, characters' thoughts and intentions may or may not be revealed, and how one scene relates to the next, if at all, may or may not be disclosed. The relative absence of causal connections among many of the shots, scenes, and sequences makes many episodic narratives open-ended. Viewers are left to experience what they see and hear without being given a pre-determined framework through which to form their thoughts and feelings. Not surprisingly, episodic narratives do less criterial prefocusing and so typically evoke fewer emotions based on pre-determined categories. They make room for viewers to respond to specific moments and to process what they see for what it is at a perceptually immediate level rather than what it is in some chain of causes and effects. To be clear, I am not suggesting that viewers can't ultimately reflect upon episodic narratives and find in them complex and highly intellectual themes and ideas. They can and do. The many interpretations of The Thin Red Line prove this. However, this almost always requires viewers to interpret the images and scenes metaphorically and to use some sort of theoretical framework to analyze what is present in the film itself.

I now want to examine some of the specific ways in which the episodic narrative of The Thin Red Line is constructed and identify some of its effects. I will show that the organization of the shots, scenes, and sequences makes them highly subjective. Even when the images and sounds are not tied to a particular character, they are often presented from a subjective point of view, which fosters an experience for viewers that is more perceptual and bodily than it is rational or intellectual. Viewers are less removed from what they see and hear on screen than they would be were the perspective more objective. As a consequence we are given more direct access to what is happening than would be possible to experience with a standard film utilizing a conventional style.

How does this work? Throughout the The Thin Red Line, sounds and images of nature are primary and are often presented as hyper-real. The camera work, lighting, editing, and sound design focus our attention on sensory information, which creates and conveys a sense of perceptual immediacy that prevents us from processing what we're watching in terms of an overarching narrative. Our attention is drawn to individual moments and we're given little indication of how they all fit together into an organized structure. Some viewers find this style challenging and give up on the film. Those who do not gain a unique type of perceptual, or phenomenological, access to the private subjective experience of individual soldiers and the natural world on the island. By giving priority to sensory experience and leaving much of it uninterpreted, Malick's style creates a subjective perspective that communicates what particular moments and experiences "feel like."

Consider the opening of the film. The entire sequence is atypical. There is no inciting incident and no back story. The characters are not introduced nor do we learn any of the standard information about who they are, what they're doing, or why. There are numerous shots of the Melanesian natives and of nature that serve no obvious narrative function. There is no apparent conflict or dramatic question raised. And the initial voiceover, itself non-narrative and reflective, is spoken by someone who never appears in the film.[5]

The introduction of Private Witt (Jim Caviezel) marks the first time the film focuses on a character. As Witt talks to a young mother holding her child, we find out almost nothing about him other than that he is "army." This brief interaction is still quite moving, less because of what the two characters say to one another than because of their facial expressions and the way that they look at one another. While it's possible to try to infer what they are thinking and feeling, many viewers will have a contagion response, reacting directly to the characters' expressions of feeling rather than to some theoretical speculation about them.

Through subsequent shots of Witt interacting with the natives, we gain a vivid sense of how Witt perceives his surroundings, and yet we still don't find out who he is, why he's on the island, or what he wants until eleven minutes into the film, a long time by traditional filmmaking standards. Nevertheless, we get a vivid sense of Witt's subjective experience of the world. We come to understand at a perceptual and affective level how he sees things, how he hears them, and how he feels about them.

As Witt recalls his mother dying, we get a flashback. Frequently flashbacks, especially those that occur early in a film, serve as exposition, telling a story within the story that reveals crucial background information or characters' motivations and desires. Witt's flashback is nothing like this; it's a meditation on immortality accompanied by a mix of voices, images, sounds, and music. The combination creates an evocative series of impressionistic images but it's not a story. Instead of a series of causally related events, we get a single event and the visual and aural associations it has for Witt. Much is left unexplained. Who is the girl in the memory? Is she even real? What was Witt doing when he had this experience and how did he react to it at the time? These sorts of questions remain unanswered. All we get are associations among particular thoughts, images, sounds, and feelings.

The structure of the opening sequence is equally unconventional. Directors, cinematographers, and editors are all typically very attentive to presenting visual information so as to make the spatial geography of a scene clear to the viewers. They want there to be no confusion about where characters are in relation to one another. When Witt begins reflecting upon his mother's death, it's clear that he is talking to someone, but we don't know to whom. When we learn that it's another soldier, Private Hoke (Will Wallace), we still don't know how the two characters are related spatially and thus who is on the right and who is on the left.

When Witt says, "I heard people talking about immortality but I ain't seen it . . .," he is looking screen right. According to the rules of filmmaking, this means Hoke must be looking screen left. Otherwise, the two characters won't look like they're talking to each other when we cut back and forth between them. Whether we realize that this is how filmmaking works or not, it's what we're expecting to see. Since Witt is looking screen right, we imagine that the character to whom he's talking will be looking screen left. But when we cut to Hoke, he is looking screen right as well.

If this scene were presented according to conventional standards, we would know the spatial geography. We don't. There's no "two shot" to orient us and thus the only information we have is the characters' eye lines.[6] In the absence of a "two shot," eye lines tell viewers how characters are related in space. In this case, both characters are looking screen right but we are led to believe that they are looking at each other. In this scene it doesn't matter that there's spatial ambiguity. In any scene in a traditional narrative film, even a conversation at a table at a diner, understanding the spatial relationships is essential to our being able to watch and process a scene. By traditional narrative filmmaking standards, Malick's formal choice here is an error. But it's not an error and, more importantly, it doesn't feel like an error. Why? Because the sequence is not structured according to a standard narrative structure. It's not about causal relationships or the pushing forward of the plot and thus it doesn't bother us or negatively impact us. On the contrary, it helps to focus our attention on the immediate experience of the characters and to heighten our awareness of what's happening in each moment.

The formal style of the opening sequence distinguishes the The Thin Red Line from most Hollywood films by organizing the narrative episodically rather than erotetically and by presenting much of it from a subjective perspective. The sequence evokes a wide range of feelings yet many of these are either non-cognitive or minimally cognitive. Without an overarching narrative the images often create a mood rather than a standard emotional response, and since the narrative provides minimal information about the characters and their relationships to one another, viewers respond more to characters' facial expressions and perceptions. In sum, viewers' response to the opening of the film is more experiential than intellectual.

Camera movement

The camera movement in *The Thin Red Line* is another central feature of its stylistic signature. In this section of the essay, I consider how specific filmmaking techniques influence viewers' experience, and, more specifically, how camera movement contributes to the creation of a subjective perspective and both expresses and elicits feelings of chaos and disorientation. Due to features of our psychology, camera movement can trigger reactions that are immediate and automatic.

Moving the camera in relation to the actors and events in specific ways and at specific speeds is one of the most reliable methods filmmakers have for directing viewers' attention and influencing their affective and perceptual experience. We naturally notice movement in the environment and when viewing a film, our attention will be drawn to movement before anything else. In *The Thin Red Line*, Malick and the film's Academy Award-winning cinematographer John Toll purposefully incorporate a number of different types of movement to elicit particular feelings and associations.[7] During the early part of the film shoot, Malick and Toll used traditional camera work, setting up a stationary camera to record choreographed actions and events. Stationary camera work tends to give filmmakers a great deal of control over many aspects of a given shot or scene, allowing them to determine what the camera records and how it is recorded in deliberate ways that can be repeated in multiple takes. In spite of the control afforded by the stationary camera, Malick and Toll were unhappy with the results, which they felt appeared "staged" and overly manipulated. They began taking a looser approach that relied less on fixed conditions. For example, they became unconcerned with getting traditional coverage and instead let the camera operators follow different actors, focusing on the "emotional thread" of different scenes rather than on pre-determined shots (Pizzello 1999: 2).

The effects of Malick and Toll's looser approach are many. Like many of the techniques used in the opening sequence, it creates a more subjective point of view that conveys individual characters' unique awareness and experience of the war and the environment. Without the traditional erotetic narrative formula to organize our experience, we are repeatedly forced to focus on the present (in the story or diegetic world), without any knowledge of how it relates to the moments that have come before, to those that will come after, or to the story in general.

It stands to reason that if Malick and Toll had been attempting to generate viewer emotion through standard means, such as criterial pre-focusing, they would not have given the camera operators such freedom since they would have needed to keep viewers' attention focused on images that would convey plot points. By allowing the camera instead to focus on the emotional thread of a scene, they create a formal style that encourages contagion and mood responses, which do not rely on cognitive evaluations of what's happening in the story.

Not all of the camera movement used in the film reflects the looser approach; some of it is highly controlled. Even when it is controlled, however, the effect is often still that the scenes and sequences are presented from a subjective or impressionistic point of view. One of the most compelling sequences in the film occurs when the soldiers from Charlie Company attempt to ascend a grassy hill in order to overtake the Japanese soldiers guarding a key airfield. As the soldiers try to make their way up the hill, the camera pushes forward, moving smoothly through the waist-high grass and shooting the landscape from low angles so that the camera's perspective reflects the eye-level perspective that the soldiers would have (Figure 7). These shots appear to be dolly shots. Due to the uneven terrain of the location, it would have been impossible to lay track for a dolly. Toll was able to adapt to these conditions by using an Akela crane. The 6000-pound Akela crane has an extremely long, 72-foot arm, which has far less of an arc than conventional crane arms. Toll installed the crane on the sides of the hills by building substantial

Figure 7

platforms. This enabled him to get the camera into places where neither a dolly track nor Steadicam could have been used (Pizzello 1999: 2).

The Akela crane allows for a vivid sense of subjective movement, which enables us to observe the events in the story world from an almost uncomfortably close distance that fixes our attention and heightens our feelings of tension. Though this perceptual perspective is subjective and particular, it is not associated with any one individual character and, as a result, we have a more immediate sensory experience than we otherwise might. Since most subjective point of view shots in traditional Hollywood films are associated with specific characters, we typically experience them in relation to those characters and so filmmakers cut back and forth between shots of the landscape from the eye level of a certain character and the face of the soldier or soldiers whose perspective we're meant to attach to the shots. This doesn't prevent us from having a vicarious experience of the story's events but in many cases it creates some degree of distance between us and the story world since we associate what we're experiencing with a specific character and with that character's particular goals and desires and the relationship between those goals and desires and the broader narrative structure.

The buffer isn't there in *The Thin Red Line*, and consequently the film depicts a direct, unmediated experience—one that is more phenomenological than narrative. As the camera moves forward, we have no time to process what's happening in relation to some organized structure. We have no time to try to answer the question of what all of it means as we are swept up—literally and figuratively—in what's happening at the particular moment in the story.

Malick and Toll also relied on Steadicam for several sequences. Steadicam is an alternative to the more traditional use of a dolly or crane for creating smooth camera movement. The Steadicam apparatus mounts the camera directly to the body of the camera operator. The camera is mounted to a pivoting arm that is itself mounted to a weight-distributing harness worn by the operator. By this means, the camera is stabilized, and the operator can move the camera in any direction in a two dimensional plane with minimal incidental camera movement. In other words, it permits elaborate camera moves with minimal "bobs and weaves," resulting in an image that, even when moving, appears steady, hence the name "Steadicam."

Hand-held camera work, on the other hand, is a technique borrowed from documentary filmmaking, where the camera operator places the camera body on his or her shoulder. There is no additional apparatus for stabilizing the camera. The result is an image with moderate to extreme incidental camera movement, that is, "bobs and weaves." The degree of incidental camera movement is typically a function of the weight of the camera, the strength and skill of the operator, and the focal length of the lens. Generally, the lighter the camera, the stronger and more skilled the operator, and the shorter the focal length of the lens, the more stable hand-held camera work will appear.

A recent trend in Hollywood filmmaking is to make the filmmaking techniques, particularly the camera work, explicit; that is, to highlight the techniques in the shooting of the film so that viewers are aware of them. All formal techniques have the potential to distract viewers from the story by diverting their attention from the story to "how the story is being told." Filmmakers can attempt to control for this, however, through their selection and combination of techniques. Malick and Toll wanted the freedom of movement provided by Steadicam and hand-held camera work but did not want the techniques to be too noticeable to viewers. They wanted to allow the camera to explore and to be more free form than it would normally be but without drawing any unnecessary attention to itself. Toll explains that his goal was to "to use the fluid, mobile camera movement as part of the overall style of the film, but in a way that supported the story" (Pizzello 1999: 2).

Unlike much of the hand-held and Steadicam work in contemporary Hollywood film, especially that used for battle or war scenes, the shooting style employed in *The Thin Red Line* doesn't distract from the content of the film or draw attention to itself. On the contrary, it allows for a more direct connection between the viewer and the events on screen by making form and content seamless. We see this in the sequence of the Americans taking over the Japanese camp. The sequence was shot primarily with Steadicam and much of it was improvised by the actors. During different takes, the Steadicam operator followed different characters through the camp. With Steadicam, the camera itself remains stable as it moves throughout the environment, but the movement of the camera through the story world is minimally controlled, generating a frenetic feeling both on screen and in the viewers but one which gets associated with the events in the story and not the presentation of those events (Pizzello 1999: 2).

Once again we get a relatively uninterpreted version of what's happening; the formal presentation of the film doesn't specify how everything fits together or what role each moment plays in some big picture. Instead, images and sounds emerge from every direction, orienting us to the immediate perceptual experience of the characters yet overwhelming and disorienting us with respect to some pre-determined plot structure. The camera work in this scene is essential for expressing and evoking the experience of chaos and unpredictability. Although viewers are likely to experience some standard emotions during this scene, they almost certainly also experience automatic affective responses to the frenetic pace of images and sounds before them.

Toll and Malick created this chaotic atmosphere without much hand-held camera work, which they relied on far less than Steadicam. Many filmmakers and television directors today use hand-held camera work to suggest a feeling of reality and instability. Take for example *The Blair Witch Project* (Daniel Myrick and Eduardo Sanchez 1999), which was considered groundbreaking when it was released for its heavy reliance on very noticeable hand-held camera work that was thought to give the film an explicitly first-person feel. Since hand-held cameras were originally used in the shooting of documentaries, we have come to associate incidental camera motion with greater reality. On one level, this makes sense since the filmmaking itself is less invisible and thus the events are presented as "presented." On another level, however, the "reality" of the story world is disrupted since our attention is shifted from the story to how it is being told and thus to the fact that it is a story.

Toll and Malick were attempting to create a different kind of aesthetic effect. Although the soldiers' experience is presented in a natural and immediate way that incorporates lots of movement in the shots, we do not attend to the filmmaking and so rather than focusing on the unstable shaky incidental camera movement we notice the instability of the story world itself and gain a vivid sensory awareness of what is unfolding in the story. Our affective engagement in this case is not interrupted or altered by the cinematic techniques.

Lighting and color

In this section of the chapter, I consider the contribution of the lighting techniques used in *The Thin Red Line* to the film's formal style and explain some of the ways this influences viewers' experience. A film's cinematographer (or director of photography) designs, plans, and controls the lighting conditions during shooting. All lighting conditions, whether natural or man-made, have an inherent *contrast ratio*. The contrast ratio of an image is the relation between the amount of light falling on the brightest part of the image and the amount of light falling on the darkest part of an image, expressed as a ratio. In a daytime exterior scene, with no cloud cover, and no supplemental artificial lighting, the contrast ratio of an image can easily reach 100:1 or greater. That is to say, one hundred times more light falls on the brightest part of the image than falls on the darkest part of the image.

All film stocks have an inherent *latitude*. The latitude of a film stock is a measure of how much contrast the film stock can represent. A film stock "represents" contrast by maintaining a linear logarithmic relationship between two variables—*exposure*: the amount of light falling on the film negative; and *density*: the opacity of the image on the film negative. Hence the latitude of a film stock is expressed as a "D log e curve," which is a fancy way of saying the relationship between the amount of light falling on the film negative and the resultant opacity of the film negative, which is both proportional and exponential. To use an analogy from sound, the latitude of a film stock is like the dynamic range of an audio format. In fact, the latitude of a film stock is sometimes referred to as the dynamic range of the film.

Not all film stocks have the same latitude. A typical film stock might be able to represent a contrast ratio of 30:1. Some film stocks can represent much more contrast than others. But all film stocks have a limit to the amount of contrast they can accommodate. When a film stock is exposed beyond its contrast limits, the result is simply that information is lost. Areas of different brightness in the image will not be represented as different opacities on the film negative. Similarly, areas of different darkness in the image will not be represented as different opacities on the film negative. Or more simply, when a film stock is pushed too far, white things won't look any whiter, and black things won't look any blacker.

When the contrast ratio of a scene exceeds the latitude of the film stock, the cinematographer is presented with a choice. He can either change the contrast ratio of the scene with supplemental artificial lighting, or expose for selective parts of the image. If he does the first, he will either cut the amount of light falling into the brightest parts of the image, or augment the amount of light falling into the darkest parts of the image, or both. He will, in other words, "cut the highlights" or "fill the shadows." If the cinematographer elects not to use supplemental artificial lighting, then he must expose for the parts of the image that are important, where what's important is typically determined by what the subject of the shot is. "Exposing for" a particular part of the image is a matter of selecting an f-stop (a measurement of the aperture size of the iris of the lens) that will determine how much light falls onto the film negative. Under conditions where the contrast ratio of the scene exceeds the latitude of the film stock, some of the image will either "fall away" or be "blown out." Although information is lost in the process, this can often be used to great cinematic effect. For example, it is the inherent limit in the latitude of film stocks that makes possible the silhouette.

The contrast ratio of the light can have a major impact on the mood of a scene and the affective experience the scene arouses. The higher the ratio, the brighter the highlights, the darker the shadows, and the "moodier" the scene will feel. The contrast ratio determines what we see in the image and what we don't, as well as the way in which we see things or how clearly we see things.

High contrast images are often, though not always, organized in one of two ways. Either the foreground can be bright while the background is dark or the background can be bright and the foreground dark. If the foreground is a human subject and the background is the set (or the story world), which is typically the case, then the subject is bright and the world is dark. This has the effect of highlighting the subject through tonal separation. Alternatively, if the background is bright and the subject is dark, the world is highlighted through tonal separation and we get silhouette. However, if the subject is moving, the movement supersedes the tonal separation that the silhouette has created. In this case, the movement of the figure will be emphasized rather than any characteristic of the figure. In sum: adjusting the contrast ratio of a scene enables the filmmakers to selectively communicate visual information to the viewer, emphasizing and de-emphasizing through tonal separation.

The Thin Red Line incorporates lots of "contrasty" images. One of the most standard uses of high contrast lighting occurs early in the film when we first see Sergeant Welsh (Sean Penn) talking to Private Witt in the belly of the troop transport ship. The appearance of this scene differs

Figure 8

greatly from what has just come before it. All of the scenes preceding it—except for Witt's memories—have been daylight exteriors of nature, of the Melanesian natives, and of Witt and Hoke with the natives. These almost all appear to be shot under natural light conditions with relatively uniform exposure from background to foreground. As a result, the subjects have appeared integrated in their environment. Stylistically and visually, the world has been as important as the people in it.

The interrogation scene between Welsh and Witt in the ship marks a significant stylistic shift. It is shot in high contrast under non-natural light conditions, and the colors are very desaturated. Lit like a film noir, this scene is dark and foreboding and thus completely unlike the scenes of nature we have just seen. The formal choices create minimally detailed images in which the world appears far less relevant than the characters. This is especially noticeable during an early close-up of Witt. Although Witt has been in more of the scenes than any other character up to this point in the film, this is the first time that he appears as an individual who is visually isolated from the background (Figure 8).

Although the use of high contrast lighting in the scene between Welsh and Witt is traditional, other uses of it in the film are far less so. The contrast ratio of many of the exterior shots of the soldiers in the jungle is very high. Since the interior scene between Welsh and Witt was shot under artificial light conditions, Toll had enormous control over how the images would look. The exterior shots are far less controlled. The natural light conditions at the shooting location for The Thin Red Line were either sunny with high contrast or overcast with softer contrast.

Very often, filmmakers deal with the unpredictability of natural light conditions and the lack of control created by low light levels in natural light conditions by putting up silks and using artificial lights to balance things out. Toll chose to shoot most of the scenes without these devices. Initially he brought lights into the jungle to light the scenes but he disliked the way the artificial light altered the natural light conditions, which created lots of natural contrast due to how the sun filtered through the trees, creating lots of highlights. (Pizzello 1999: 3).

By shooting under these conditions, Toll ended up with many scenes where the actors' faces would be detailed while the background would be very bright and burned out. Thus, selected parts of some images either "fell away" or were "blown out" because of the highlights. Lots of visual information in these scenes is therefore missing and the world appears more impressionistic and less clearly defined than we're used to seeing, especially in a war movie. Toll went with the natural conditions because they made the images seem out of control and created a sense of visual chaos to match the feelings of chaos and powerlessness of the soldiers. The form matches the content in these scenes and helps to create a visual image for viewers that corresponds to the subjective experience of soldiers. Another way to think about this is that the style of these scenes provides impressionistic images that convey the subjective or phenomenological experience of the soldiers. If the scenes had been lit so as to correct for the natural imbalance of light, there would have been more visual information recorded and a greater sense of control created. The latter style would have corresponded more to a third person point of view that is recording events not as they are experienced by embodied individuals in the natural world but rather as they could be seen by some perfect omniscient camera.

Conclusion

In this essay, I have attempted to shed light on certain features of the relationship between the cinematic style in *The Thin Red Line* and the type of experience the film evokes. I focused my analysis on three of the film's formal features: first, a highly subjective perspective; second, impressionistic images and feelings; and third, an episodic narrative. My goal in explaining the techniques Malick and the other filmmakers employed to create these aesthetic characteristics was to show how and why film influences viewers' attention, perception, and feelings. Until we understand more about this, we can't begin to theorize at a higher level about what the film "means."

I covered aspects of narrative structure, camera movement, and lighting but much more can be said about the form of The Thin Red Line and viewers' responses to it; my examination has barely scratched the surface. I said nothing, for example, about the sound design or the score of the film, both of which are extraordinarily important for its overall style and its ability to affect viewers. Much remains to be explored.

My essay has been fairly technical with all the talk of cognitive and non-cognitive affects, erotetic and episodic narration, the Akela crane, Steadicam, and contrast ratios. This may strike some readers as ironic given the lyrical quality of The Thin Red Line. It strikes me that way. After all, films are meant to be experienced, not analyzed into minutiae. Malick's films, in particular, provide opportunities for deeply meaningful experiential engagement. Nevertheless, I hope that my examination will help viewers to understand why The Thin Red Line is such a powerful film and how it achieves some of its effects, and will provide a basis on which to build interpretations of the film's meaning. While philosophy is typically less engaging than film, philosophical analysis has the potential to greatly enhance our understanding of film and our relationship to it, which can make our experiences of film even more meaningful and more engaging.[8]

Notes

1   For an overview of some of the standard interpretations, See David Davies 2008, in this collection.
2   For a helpful discussion of moods and the relationship between art and moods, see Carroll (2003).
3   The estimated budget of The Thin Red Line was fifty-two million dollars. Alongside several unknown actors, it featured several big name stars, including Sean Penn, John Travolta, and George Clooney. (Budget information from IMDb-Pro, a subscription-only internet database, which is a wholly owned subsidiary of Amazon.com and provides detailed information on movies and the movie industry, is available at http://pro.imdb.com/).
4   Carroll 1999: 31–2. Much more can be said about Carroll's account. This is a brief overview.
5   It should be noted that the person speaking in this voiceover sounds a great deal like Private Witt (Jim Caviezel), who has a number of voiceovers during

the film. It's likely that the filmmakers intended viewers to attribute the voiceover to Witt. However, the voice is not actually Jim Caviezel's (Sandhya Shardanand, assistant to Terrence Malick, private communication).

6 A "two-shot" refers to a shot featuring two characters. Two-shots can be used to establish the spatial geography of a scene. "Eye line" refers to the direction the actor is looking off screen. In order to achieve continuity, the absence of which distracts viewers, the eye lines of actors whose characters are talking to one another need to match.

7 Toll has twice won the Oscar for Best Cinematography, first for Legends of the Fall.

8 An early version of this essay was presented as part of a panel on Terrence Malick's films at the 2007 Pacific Division meeting of the American Society for Aesthetics. I would like to thank the audience for a very useful discussion. I would also like to thank Ryan Nichols and Tobyn DeMarco whose comments and support made this essay far better, and Sandhya Shardanand for answering questions no one else could have. I am indebted to Bryon Cunningham for sharing his expertise on filmmaking and "structure" and for introducing me to Malick's films. Finally, I am enormously grateful to David Davies who inspired me to write this chapter, provided invaluable feedback at every stage, and exhibited superhuman levels of patience with me. He "gets it."

References

Carroll, N. (1999) "Film, emotion, and genre," in C. Plantinga and G.M. Smith (eds), Passionate Views, Baltimore, MD: The Johns Hopkins University Press.

—— (2003) "Art and mood: preliminary notes and conjectures," The Monist, 86 (4): 521–55.

—— (2008) The Philosophy of Motion Pictures, Malden, MA: Wiley-Blackwell.

Coplan, A. (2006) "Catching characters' emotions," Film Studies: An International Review 8: 26–38.

Davies, D. (2008) "Vision, touch, and embodiment in The Thin Red Line," in this volume, 45–64.

Hatfield, E., J.T. Cacioppo, and R.L. Rhapson (1992) Emotional Contagion, Cambridge: Cambridge University Press.

LeDoux, J. (1998) The Emotional Brain: The Mysterious Underpinnings of Emotional Life, New York: Touchstone.

Nussbaum, M. (2004) "Emotions as judgments of value and importance," in R.C. Solomon (ed.), Thinking and Feeling: Contemporary Philosophers on Emotion, New York: Oxford University Press.

Pizzello, S. (1999) "The war within," American Cinematographer (Feb. 1999), http://www.theasc.com/magazine/feb99/war/index.htm (accessed September 10, 2007), 3.

Prinz, J. (2004) *Gut Reactions: A Perceptual Theory of Emotion*, New York: Oxford University Press.

Robinson, J. (1995) "Startle," *The Journal of Philosophy*, XCII, 2: 53–74.

—— (2005) *Deeper than Reason: Emotion and its Role in Literature, Music, and Art*, New York: Oxford University Press.

Smith, M. (1995) *Engaging Characters: Fiction, Emotion, and the Cinema*, New York: Oxford University Press.

Solomon, R.C. (2004) "Emotions, thoughts, and feelings: emotions as engagements with the world," in R.C. Solomon (ed.), *Thinking and Feeling: Contemporary Philosophers on Emotion*, New York: Oxford University Press.

Chapter 6

Iain Macdonald

NATURE AND THE WILL TO POWER IN TERRENCE MALICK'S *THE NEW WORLD*

Immer zerreißet den Kranz des Homer und zählet die Väter
Des vollendeten ewigen Werks!
Hat es doch *eine* Mutter nur und die Züge der Mutter,
Deine unsterblichen Züge, Natur.

Schiller

A community of being?

ONE OF THE MOST FREQUENTLY discussed issues in the literature on Terrence Malick's films is the problem of nature or, more specifically, his portrayal of the relation of human beings to nature—from the arid landscapes of *Badlands* (1973) and the locusts of *Days of Heaven* (1978) to the jungle of *The Thin Red Line* (1998).[1] The same is true of *The New World*, initially released in 2005 in a 150-minute version, then cut to 135 minutes and re-released in January of 2006. Indeed, Malick's interest in nature seems to come across more directly in *The New World* than in any of his other films, with the possible exception of *The Thin Red Line*. Or, to put it another way, *The New World* makes even more explicit something that is also present, but to varying degrees, in his earlier work, namely, the "nature" of human nature.

In interpreting *The New World*, however, it has to be acknowledged that it was not an overnight critical success. Nor was it an overwinter success, although J. Hoberman (2006) eventually wrote in *The Village Voice* that the film seemed to be gaining momentum, ever so slowly, as a cult masterpiece, destined for midnight showings in trendy arts cinemas (a good thing on the whole, albeit somewhat backhanded as a compliment aimed at revealing the film's strengths). In short, the film split the critics in the entertainment industry. Few were those who unqualifiedly praised Malick's uninterrupted genius, and even among Malick supporters there were often moments of perplexity or reserve. For example, one critic (Burr 2006) called the film an "exhausting, astounding drama" adding that it is at once "self-indulgent, gorgeous, maddening, gruelling, [and] ultimately transcendent"—and that is from the pen of a Malick yea-sayer. As regards the question of nature, another critic—this time from the camp of Malick skeptics—summed up her objections by saying: "Terrence Malick may not care much for people, but he never met a tree he didn't like" (Zacharek 2006). It remains unclear whether she knew just how right she was in saying this—though not in the way she intended—for Malick does indeed seem to offset human drama against the workings of nature, as we shall see below. One way or the other, this complaint, or versions of it, comes back again and again in the reviews of the film. Presumably, the problem has to do with the long, speculative shots of water, grasslands, marshes, forests, fungus, insects, and so on that make up the film, punctuated by the dialogue and action that many people might expect to be more prominent. Similar criticisms were voiced when *The Thin Red Line* was released, reaching their most extreme point, perhaps, when one commentator denounced Malick's cinema as "metaphysical gas," complaining that the narrative and human elements in the film were, for Malick, merely "a place to play with his philosophical conundrums about nature and our relationship to it" (Whalen 1999: 163, 165). Once again, the disbelievers may be onto something with such comments, though they tend to tackle the problem from the wrong end of things, often from the standpoint of all too traditional expectations and skepticism about film as a medium for philosophical reflection.

By contrast, a small handful of writers have directly confronted Malick's purported metaphysics and the "problem of nature." The voiceover from the opening moments of *The Thin Red Line* is a common starting point for such reflections: "What's this war in the heart of nature? Why does nature vie with itself? The land contend with the sea? Is there an avenging power in nature? Not one power, but two?" Some of these more detailed reflections—often drawing on a perceived Heideggerianism in Malick's films (see, for example, Furstenau and MacAvoy 2003)—are important and insightful. But it is not at all clear that Malick is (or why he should be) interested in remaining faithful to his original philosophical interest in Heidegger.[2] Thus while the metaphysical question of "the nature of human nature" is surely Malick's central concern as a director, these preliminary investigations should be tested against other evidence presented (often obliquely) in his films. What comes across in The New World, specifically, is a kind of naturalism that can be articulated beyond strictly Heideggerian concerns.

In this vein, Simon Critchley quite rightly underscores the indifference and blindness of nature in The Thin Red Line when he writes: "nature's indifference to human purposes follows from a broadly naturalistic conception of nature. Things are not enchanted in Malick's universe, they simply *are*, and we are things too. They are remote from us and continue on regardless of our strivings."[3] Things merely *are*, for Malick; no doubt this is what explains all the trees, but what are the specific features of this naturalism? What is the specific sense of things continuing on "regardless of" our strivings, especially if we are truly things too, implicated in nature's indifference? In a similar vein, Leo Bersani and Ulysse Dutoit argue that The Thin Red Line asks us "to do little more than to let the world be" (2004: 164). They add to this that in order to let the world be, the subject must be divested of its subjectivity, must become anonymous (i.e., by bracketing "strivings" specific to individuals), in order to replicate both "the world as an accretion to consciousness, and a look, ceaselessly receptive to the world" (2004: 165). Thus the idea is that consciousness *constitutes* the world as it, in turn, is *constituted* by the world. This then leads them to conclude that Malick's vision of nature and human life involves a "community of all being," that is, an implication in the world and a togetherness that "makes no essential distinction between the human and the non-human" (2004: 171).

These interpretations concur on the central point: the nature of human nature involves a kind of community in which human striving is inherently a part of, and framed by, natural indifference—where indifference is ambiguously understood as either blindness or non-differentiatedness. But the details of Malick's all-embracing naturalism remain obscure in these readings, just as the concept of nature's indifference remains somewhat fuzzy. So while it is true that Malick's films, and *The Thin Red Line* in particular, show us nature's power and indifference, it might yet be helpful to know more about the metaphysics that underpins this view of nature. What is the specific quality of human participation in nature, according to Malick? *The New World* provides an answer to this question.

The "nature" of human nature

Most people will know that *The New World* is a retelling of the Pocahontas legend and the founding of the Jamestown settlement in Virginia in 1607. It is interesting in itself that Malick should have chosen this particular story as the narrative basis for the film, for a number of reasons—not the least of which is the rather vexing question of how his film relates to the hackneyed and romanticized Disney version of 1995, to which we shall return below. In any event, Malick's version of the story opens with a voiceover that recalls the first moments of *The Thin Red Line*, though somewhat less ominous in its content. Pocahontas (Q'Orianka Kilcher) says: "Come spirit, help us tell sing the story of our land. You are our mother. We, your field of corn. We rise from out of the soul of you." She then spreads her arms skyward before swimming and playing in the water with her friends. The viewer's first glimpse of Captain John Smith (Colin Farrell), on the other hand, the man the historical Pocahontas is supposed to have rescued from certain death, is quite different. As his ship sails up the James River, Smith too reaches skyward—while looking through the bars in the deck; he is in the brig, in chains, having made remarks construed as mutinous on the voyage over.

This seems to be a contrast central to the film. On the one hand: Pocahontas's appeal to the spirit of the land and the ease and freedom of her integration into the landscape, into the life of her community, already evident in the opening seconds of the film; on the other hand: the bedraggled and smelly, sea-weary English sailors, and especially Smith, portrayed as a prisoner in his own environment. The English are shown in this light throughout the first half of the film: uncomfortable, hungry, sick, quickly putting themselves behind the walls of the fort they are so desperate to build. The first shot of Smith in chains is indicative of this tension in all its varied forms: Pocahontas sees the sky as open and embracing, whereas Smith sees it through bars, imprisoned in the Christian Eurocentrism that will later prevent him from requiting

Pocahontas's love. Along the same lines, the film is filled with shots of interiors, but with the camera looking out, at people, animals, or just space. The interior seems to define the fundamental perspective of the English: the ship, the fort, the cottage, the church, the manor house, and so on; it is from out of these structures, reflective of their social order, that they see the world.

One cannot help but think of the opening line of Rousseau's *The Social Contract*: "Man was born free, and everywhere he is in chains." Indeed, Malick seems to be drawing attention to this apparent paradox of human society: the stark contrast between the familial bonds that characterize the native social system, and the dirty and restrictive, artificial social edifice of the English—or, alternatively, between the very different ways these two cultures relate to nature. The whole problem of the film, when seen in this light would then be to chart this tension, the starkness of the contrast between two distinct and opposed social orders. The chains Smith is in at the beginning of the film would therefore represent the chains of civilization, of which Pocahontas is free, at least at first. Of course, one would have to add to this picture the mitigation of this dualism, as undertaken by Pocahontas in her assimilation, her baptism and eventually her marriage to John Rolfe (Christian Bale). On this reading, the logic of the film would rest on a dynamic of like and unlike, in which unlike must become like in order for the tension between the bars of the brig and the open sky to be resolved. As Pocahontas says to Smith at the beginning of her assimilation: "Am I as you like?"

Fortunately, things are never so pedestrian in Malick's films. In fact, this tidy story of cultural difference and assimilation collapses as soon as the contrasts of the opening sequence begin to unfold. Or even before. Already in the first voiceover, in which Pocahontas calls on her spirit mother to help her sing the story of her people's land, it is impossible not to hear it as an invocation of the Muse, in the manner of Homer: "Come spirit, help us tell sing the story of our land." At first, this seems to raise a thorny question: is Malick imposing a European perspective on Pocahontas and on the whole story? But to raise this sort of concern would be to miss the point by tacitly reinforcing the cultural dichotomies that Malick deconstructs in the film. It may be more fruitful, at least provisionally, to look at things the other way around: that is, by reading the invocation of the Muse as a repetition of profoundly human practices that transcend particular civilizations, of which Homer provides us with merely one version.

Thus, Pocahontas's invocation expresses a fundamentally human desire to recover, through and beyond the present, an origin of sorts or foundational meaning—in this case, the story of "our land." The invocation is in this way bound up with a radical questioning that Pocahontas herself articulates explicitly a little later in the film, when she asks herself: "Mother. Where do you live? In the sky, the clouds, the sea? Show me your face. Give me a sign." She is asking here about the *sense* of the world, of nature, and of how nature conditions her and pushes her blindly towards Smith, in spite of his foreignness and self-avowed untrustworthiness. Yet the same is true of Smith, who asks himself very similar questions early in the film; for example: "Who are you, whom I so faintly hear, who urge me ever on?" From opposed perspectives, they are nevertheless posing the same basic questions.

What they are asking themselves is what makes them human and how they should understand themselves as creatures with natural drives and passions. Of course, their questioning may seem ambiguous in the context of the narrative. Are they not asking about their love for each other? Yes, in a way, although Pocahontas's invocation and Smith's apostrophe both come *before* they fall in love. To the extent that the question of their love only arises *later*, we should perhaps already suspect that the point here is to explore the deeper question of what binds them together in *nature*—not just as would-be lovers, as the (deeply misleading) narrative would have us think. However, the claim is not that Malick ultimately denies the social reality of cultural or amorous tensions; on the contrary, he affirms it in its stark obviousness. But these tensions are clearly not his central concern; they are only an occasion for exploring the enigma of nature and human nature, instinct and reason. At this level, love and cultural difference are relegated to the status of epiphenomena or manifestations of natural processes.

To summarize: the specific differences that seem so important on the narrative level are called into question by Pocahontas's and Smith's *shared* reflections on themselves and on nature. On this reading, Pocahontas's "invocation of the Muse" is a particular expression of a need she and her people share with Smith and his: that of assuring the coherence of the community in memory and cultural practices. It is only on the level of the content of these practices, one might say, that cultural difference becomes an issue: on the specific questions of property and religion, for example. On the level of their form, they rather resemble each other. Thus the (at times very loose) cohesion of both groups is based around beliefs and motives proper to each group, but the fact that there is and can be such cohesion is *shared*: one process, but two manifestations.

Admittedly, many of the narrative elements of the film do not seem to lend themselves to this reading. After all, Smith abandons Pocahontas in part because of the cultural divide that separates them, and perhaps in part also because he wishes to pursue personal fame and fortune (as was the historical Smith's wont). But once we take the spotlight off individual characters' specific interactions, we begin to see how Malick draws out the common features of their reflections. In other words, if we bracket for a moment the "story of Pocahontas" and consider the imagery deployed by Malick, it very quickly becomes apparent that most of the contrasts that he sets up in the film can be read in the same way. For example, for every interior and every barricade set up by the English, there is a corresponding image portraying the natives' own ways of enclosing themselves in some interior, their own way of dividing sky and earth, land and sea. Consider the gunports and deck grills on the English ships and the smoke hole of the native longhouse; the doorways or window frames of the cottages and the doorway of the longhouse; the stained glass windows of the English church and the window of the native shrine; the English ships' rigging and the native fishing nets, and so on. Or in a more moral parallel, even as Smith proclaims the natives' innocence and ignorance as regards betrayal and forgiveness (thereby underscoring, he thinks, the difference between them), a moment later Pocahontas's father, King Powhatan (August Schellenberg), demands that she not betray her people: "Promise me you will put your people before all else. [. . .] Even your own heart. He [Smith] is not one of us." In spite of the chasm that separates them, then, and even in the very expression of this cultural divide, Malick insists that their difference is purely perspectival and that at root they share a common logic, a common reason that engenders their respective worlds and defines their relation to nature.

That on its own would not be the most radical claim. And it would be a rather ambiguous claim, hovering indecisively between the philosophical assertion of universal subjectivity and a "New Agey"—and historically false—affirmation of universal humanity (such as we see in the Disney version of the Pocahontas story). But on the contrary, the strength of the film is that it does not stop there, that is, with the idea of a common humanity. The question is rather: what drives this common reason? Or to put it in other terms, if Malick's films attest to a "community of being," as The New World seems to illustrate so well, then we still need to know what constitutes this community beyond communities (see Bersani and Dutoit 2004: 171). The answer doubtless has to do with the relation of human reason to blind nature, which, as mentioned, is a problem that is broached by Pocahontas and Smith in the film: "Mother. Where do you live?" and "Who are you . . . who urge me ever on?" It is in the exploration of these questions (for example in the network of parallel images running through the film) that we can begin to discern Malick's metaphysics.

To anticipate somewhat on what follows: Malick's metaphysics—his community of being—involves a materialism, roughly Nietzschean in character, that denies not only cultural essentialism, but also any meaningful distinction between reason and nature. In other words, it denies the superiority or dominance of rational beings over nature by affirming the natural character of reason. The end result is that human reason turns out to be nothing more than an expression of the "blind" rationality of nature—not an exception to the rule of nature but rather its unmitigated realization. In this sense, it is not that "all is life, and life is good," as though life were eternally beautiful, good or true. This is clearly not Malick's view. On the contrary, all is struggle and conflict, a "war in the heart of nature," as in The Thin Red Line, and one in which human beings play no special role, in spite of what we might think. It is just that we have the capacity to see this war for what it is.

The key scene in The New World comes when Smith is sent upriver to find the Powhatan camp. In its simplicity, the scene summarizes Malick's view of the nature of human nature. Gradually, Smith is separated from his compatriots and his captive guides, until he is alone in the swamp, in full armour, armed only with a sword and a pistol. As Smith makes his way through the swamp, hoping to find the native camp, he is attacked from all sides by arrows and club-wielding natives. His pistol holds a single shot; he fires on one of his attackers, but they outnumber him. Once his pistol is discharged, he is left with his sword and parrying dagger (Figure 9); but encumbered as he is, he cannot prevail and is quickly taken prisoner.

Figure 9

What is the significance of this highly artificial scene, in which Smith is reduced to fighting alone in the swamp, where he is barely able to move because of the armour he is wearing? Obviously, the answer involves self-preservation—there is no other reason for the armour. But is it *strict* self-preservation that is on display here, that is, Smith's purely personal desire to stay alive? Or is Smith acting out a more basic human drama in this scene, in which the bizarre spectacle of an armour-clad soldier knee-deep in water actually illustrates something about the human condition? A passage from Theodor Adorno's *Negative Dialectics*, where Adorno is at his most Nietzschean, may shed some light on what is taking place in this scene. Adorno writes:

> The emphasis that philosophy puts on the constitutive power of the subjective moment . . . cuts us off from the truth. Species like the dinosaur triceratops or the rhinoceros haul around the armour that protects them, like a prison they grow into, and which they try in vain to shed (or so it seems, anthropomorphically). Their imprisonment in their own survival mechanism may be what explains the special ferocity of rhinoceroses, just as it explains the unacknowledged and therefore all the more terrifying ferocity of *homo sapiens*. The subjective moment is set into the objective one, as it were; but as something limiting to which the subject must submit, the subjective moment is itself objective.[4]

With characteristic dialectical verve, Adorno here describes an important aspect of his Nietzsche-inspired materialism. Essentially, the idea is that there is no use pretending that there exists some kind of heroic subjectivity that pits itself against blind nature or that is able to stand outside the world as it constitutes it. Nature and the human desire to master nature are one and the same thing. Or, more generally, consciousness and objective nature are two sides of the same coin to the extent that consciousness is a natural survival mechanism that evolved with and defines the human species. Just as the triceratops and its armour are inseparable, we, as natural creatures, and the myriad methods by which we divide and conquer nature are inseparable too. Therefore, any attempt to argue for the a priori, spiritual or categorial character of rational subjectivity ("the constitutive power of the subjective moment") is only to struggle in vain against the unbreakable hold that nature has on us: reason, our own "survival mechanism," is just the natural capacity that allows us to know and experience "external" nature. By the same token, if we exaggerate this projected externality of nature, then reason will inevitably deny its provenance—as though it were a Münchhausenian power that could lift itself out of nature, as though the gaze that the thinking subject directs towards nature were somehow *opposable* to nature. Or, to put it the other way around, it is important for understanding the nature of human nature to know that it is nature—in the form of reason—that (paradoxically) "allows" us to experience nature as something "external." Thus, we, as knowers and doers, are caught in a web of natural possibility, and every effort to remove ourselves from this web only results in further entanglement. We cannot disentangle reason from nature because their entwinement is precisely what makes us the creatures we are. Indeed, one might say that nature has made us what we must be to survive, precisely by making us "rational"; and yet, reason is what also makes us experience nature as foreign and as menacing, as threatening our survival. We cannot escape this predicament, but we can at least adopt a perspective that does not muddle the problem: reason must be seen as nothing more than an incredibly adaptable and therefore powerful natural survival mechanism. It is in this sense that the classic emphasis on a priori, constitutive subjective rationality is false. The subjective rational "core" of human subjectivity is not a priori at all, but rather an expression of what is supposed to be distinct from pure reason, that is, "objective" nature.

Adorno derives these ideas from his (dialectical) interpretation of Nietzsche, for whom "the human being is a creature that constructs

rhythms and forms; there is nothing else in which he is more expert."[5]
This capacity to construct forms, to see patterns, rhythms or, in short,
the ability to see identity in difference, is what we normally think of as
the essence of the human being, as defined by Aristotle. We are supposed
to be rational animals and, moreover, the *only* rational animal.[6] This latter
claim is essentially what Nietzsche's materialism denies. As he says:
"'Thinking' in its basic state (taken pre-organically) is *establishing forms*
[*Gestalten-Durchsetzen*], like crystals. What is *essential* in our way of thinking
is the classification of new material according to old patterns (= the
Procrustean bed), *imposing* identity on the new."[7]

Simplistically, thought is reducible to natural accretion and assimilation. Consequently, we are fundamentally no "better" than the crystal
or the amoeba. Indeed, like the amoeba, in another of Nietzsche's
examples, the basic operations of reason amount to the assimilation or
rejection of matter, that is, positing conceptual distinctions that include
and exclude, assimilate like to like by excluding unlike: "All thinking,
judging and perceiving, understood as *comparing* [*Vergleichen*], presupposes
positing equality [*Gleichsetzen*] or, in earlier times, a *levelling* [*Gleichmachen*].
'Levelling' is just what the amoeba does when it assimilates appropriated
matter."[8] From the standpoint of nature, then, it makes absolutely no
difference whether this process occurs on the level of satisfying natural
desires, of propagating a religion or a worldview, or of engaging in
scientific research. Strictly speaking, the differences between the human
being, the amoeba, and the crystal are only differences of degree—and
perhaps not even that in light of the death of God.[9]

Nietzsche adds to this that so-called external reality is, for all of these
reasons, exhausted by the sum of the judgments we make about it, that
is, the sum of the identities we naturally impose on the sheer difference at the heart of nature; such judgments are, after all, "fragments" of
nature thinking itself. But then external reality is not really "external" at
all if the way we perceive and conceive nature is inevitably an expression of nature. In other words, whether our judgments are "exact" or
"true to reality" is quite beside the point if we cannot rigorously
distinguish between the amoeba and ourselves or between "inner" and
"outer" nature. Ultimately, this boils down to a single thought: knowledge does not serve truth; it serves preservation. As Nietzsche puts it:
"what is most important is the inexactness and indefiniteness [of our

judgments], which allow for a certain *simplification of the external world,* which [in turn] is precisely the sort of intellectual activity [*Intelligenz*] that favours preservation [*Erhaltung*]."[10]

Coming back now to Smith, alone in the swamp in full armour, we can see better how Malick moves through and beyond the cultural tensions he sets up in *The New World.* Heavily armoured, Smith carries with him into the foreignness of the swamp his entire culture and its outlook on nature. Like the fort his men build to protect themselves, the armour is the mark of the Old World and its emphasis on heroic subjectivity and human dominion—which is an expression of nature in *denial* of nature. (Denial is not just a river in Egypt, as the joke goes.) In other words, the Old World emphasis on subjective rationality is part of what allowed and allows it to flourish, a sum of mechanisms and patterns of thought that meet natural conditions of existence.[11] Of course, the armour is also the symbol of the Old World's mastery of nature (metallurgy and military strength) coming into conflict with the New World's very different relation to nature. But the technical accomplishments of the Old World are only as good as the environment and the interpretation of the environment that produced them and led to an understanding of needs and how to meet them. In the swamp, the nimbler, unencumbered natives easily defeat the inappropriately clad Englishman.

In other words, the armour as such does not give us a criterion of superiority or "fitness" for survival. The armour and clothes the English wear afford them no protection against the elements as do the furs of the natives; on the other hand, the clubs and axes of the natives afford them no protection against the English guns. Their respectively approximate ways of relating to their surroundings are on a par as regards the logic of their actions. Structurally, the *generation* of these outlooks is the same. Thus whether a particular outlook involves armour, forts and gunpowder, or animal pelts, longhouses, and clubs is irrelevant to understanding the *general* relation of human beings to nature.

What we bear witness to in watching *The New World,* then, has little to do with star-crossed lovers. Likewise, it has little to do with the Old World versus the New or the portrayal of the historical colonial mindset. Of course, these are also part of the film, woven into it on a narrative level; but they are rather more coherent and convincing as occasions for reflecting upon nature than as the primary elements of the film.

Pocahontas Redux

Yet if Malick's vision of nature is comprehensible along these lines, that is, if cultural conflict and difference are nothing but an expression of nature's inexorable tyranny, then one might well wonder why the story of Pocahontas should serve as the vehicle of this apparent allegory. Indeed, if it is "mere nature" that is on display in the film, then surely the narrative runs the risk of being an arbitrary illustration of this deeper "truth" of nature. Perhaps, but it is important to underscore that Malick is no metaphysical "backworldsman" (Hinterweltler), in Nietzsche's mocking phrase, seeking hidden meanings behind or beyond the world of fleeting appearances. On the contrary, The New World asks the viewer to look upon what occurs in the narrative, on the level of appearances, from a new perspective—not as an "allegory" of nature, but rather as nature itself or, better, as nature expressing itself as reason in history. For there is nothing "behind" the narrative, strictly speaking; everything it says is held within it as an expression of what it always already is—though we may be fooled by what we see, by our viewing habits or cultural expectations. For this reason, then, the narrative is far from "arbitrary" or "dispensable," for it is the content and presentation of the narrative that disrupts our habits and expectations and that draws our attention to this question of the nature of human nature.[12] Moreover, as the narrative is articulated in the film, it does not expose something "behind" or "beyond" the action; it rather undermines its own content and so incites us to see this articulation from a new vantage point: as "nature-history," that is, as nature coalescing into history (Cf. Adorno 1984; 1997: vol. 1).

Of course, if the narrative presents us with two perspectives simultaneously—that of the story's characters and that of nature itself— then this duality must be discernible in the film. For, until now, it has only been a working hypothesis that the film in fact presents us with a quasi-Nietzschean vision of nature, based on a provisional bracketing of the narrative content of the film (the story of cultural difference in early America, or of the relationship between Pocahontas and Smith). But what justifies this act of putting the storyline out of play, in order to focus on imagery and some isolated lines of dialogue that allegedly convey a vision of nature? Part of the film's brilliance is that it does not just engage in occasional reflection on the nature of human nature; it actually incites the viewer to undertake a change of perspective on its own narrative content, thereby encouraging us to see the Pocahontas story *as* the story of nature. More specifically, *The New World* invites the viewer to follow the narrative along a path of self-deconstruction that displays the indifference and unity of nature that is at the root of what presents itself initially as its opposite: the simple but iconic tale of ill-fated lovers separated by cultural difference in the early days of colonial America. This self-deconstruction can be made clearer through a brief look at the historical genesis of the Pocahontas legend itself.

There is no doubt that the Pocahontas story is a mainstay of American lore. It was initially passed down to us in Smith's memoirs and has persisted in numerous retellings to the present day. It is understood as an archetypal moment in the history of the founding of America. However, it is also a story that has been distorted by its romanticization, possibly due, in part, to Smith's problem, as a writer, with separating fact from fiction. At any rate, many people will be aware that the historical story of Pocahontas and Smith was simplified and imbued with mythic qualities over the centuries, culminating in an execrable caricature of a caricature in 1995 with the release of Disney's animated feature film, *Pocahontas*. In relation to this latter point, the Disney version not only tells the story in its most popular form, but further distorts it by imposing a love interest between Pocahontas and Smith that even the real Smith could never have invented (in point of fact, Smith nowhere suggests that he and Pocahontas were romantically involved). Roughly, the story is as follows: in the early days of the founding of Jamestown, Smith is captured by Powhatan and about to be executed when Pocahontas, who is supposed to be in love with Smith, throws herself on him and successfully pleads for his life. But while no one should be surprised by Disney's distortion of history in the name of love, it is utterly astonishing at first blush that Malick should tell this version of it. Why did Malick choose to present us with a fictional love story so close in content to the cliché-ridden Disney version of the story?

Of course, neither Malick nor Disney bears responsibility for the reception and mythologization of Smith's experience in Virginia in the early seventeenth century. That Pocahontas and Smith were involved romantically was an invention of nineteenth-century popular adaptations; but it is Smith himself who is ultimately responsible for the fictionalization of his experiences. As related in the 1624 *Generall historie of Virginia*,

New-England and the Summer Isles . . ., he describes the core of the Pocahontas story as follows:

> having feasted [Smith] after their best barbarous manner they could, a long consultation was held, but the conclusion was, two great stones were brought before Powhatan: then as many as could layd hands on him, dragged him to them, and thereon laid his head, and being ready with their clubs, to beate out his braines, Pocahontas the Kings dearest daughter, when no intreaty could prevaile, got his head in her armes, and laid her owne upon his to save him from death: whereat the Emperour was contented he should live to make him hatchets and her bells, beads, and copper; for they thought him as well of all occupations as themselves. . . . Two dayes after, Powhatan . . . came unto him and told him now they were friends. . . .
>
> Smith 1986b: 151

It is this short passage that is the principal basis for all later re-tellings, including Malick's and Disney's. At first, it seems to establish the historical event at the origin of the Pocahontas legend. But there are a number of problems with Smith's account that make it difficult to accept what he says at face value.

In the first instance, the account is uncorroborated, since it takes place when Smith is alone in captivity in the Powhatan camp. But more problematically, as has been underscored by detractors since the seventeenth century, it seems that Smith the "historian" was at best a mere raconteur and at worst a brazen liar. In fact, given the inconsistencies in Smith's own retellings of the rescue by Pocahontas, taken within the greater context of numerous implausible exploits recounted in his memoirs, many have simply dismissed Smith as a self-aggrandizing fabricator.[13] Indeed, it is hard to explain why Smith waits until 1624 to include a detailed account of the "rescue" episode in the story of his captivity in the final days of 1607. Perhaps that on its own would not be very damning; there is nothing very peculiar in the fact that Smith's memoirs date from a much later period. However, *The Generall historie* of 1624 is not the first record of this period from Smith's hand. In 1612, in *The Proceedings of the English colonie in Virginia*, Smith fails to mention Pocahontas and relates a very different version of his captivity and release: "A month those Barbarians kept him prisoner, many strange triumphes and conjurations they made of him, yet hee so demeaned himselfe amongst them, as he not only diverted them from surprising the Fort, but procured his owne liberty . . ." (Smith 1986c: 213). These two very different accounts leave little room for reconciliation: for either Smith rescued himself or was rescued. In any case, Pocahontas's name does not appear in the passage. It is therefore understandable that such an inconsistency should have led critics to claim that Smith's later version was invented. And indeed, if that were so, then *anything* could have happened to the stalwart Captain Smith, the daring traveler whose incredible adventures included being captured by the Powhatan, escaping certain death, and, why not, having a local princess fall in love with him. Following this line of sensational interpretation, already partly manifest in Smith's view of himself, it is not difficult to trace the birth of the legend: Smith himself wanted to become such a legend and worked towards this goal in his writings.

However, it is worth noting that the rescue was, in fact, first mentioned by Smith in 1616, in a private letter to Queen Anne, where he writes of her that she was:

> the Kings most deare and wel-beloved daughter, being but a child of twelve or thirteene yeeres of age, whose compassionate and pitifull heart, of my desperate estate, gave me much cause to respect her. . . . After some six weeks fatting amongst those Salvage Courtiers, at the minute of my execution, she hazarded the beating out of her owne brains to save mine. . . .
>
> Smith 1986b: 259

At least here Smith mentions a rescue, though he cannot help but exaggerate the duration of his captivity.[14] Yet even so, we are still left with two conundrums. First, given the inconsistency mentioned in Smith's writings, did Pocahontas "save" him or not? And second, if she did, what authorizes Malick to repeat the hopelessly romanticized version of the story, in which Pocahontas not only saves Smith from being executed, but does so because she is in love with him?

Whether or not Smith was a truthful and reliable historian is not a question that can be answered without undertaking a long and detailed examination of his writings, comparing his accounts with those provided by others. Contemporary scholarship has done much along these lines to redeem Smith's reputation and it has been argued that there is less wilful invention than self-glorifying embellishment in his memoirs.[15] Certainly, we cannot know beyond the shadow of a doubt what happened to Smith in the Powhatan camp, and Smith's incomplete and inconsistent accounts do not help matters. At the very least, he was held and released, and at the time of his release he was regarded as a friend of the Powhatan. Of course, it may be that Smith invented the role he ascribes to Pocahontas in his letter to Queen Anne in order somehow to curry favor with the English court, but even so, he clearly remembers her from that time and other events he mentions involving her can be corroborated, such as her visits to the Jamestown Fort and various interactions between her and the fort's inhabitants (see Smith 1986a: vol. 2, 258, n.1). Thus there may be marginally more reason to believe that some sort of rescue occurred, while yet remaining skeptical about the details.

It may also be that Smith was not so much a fabulist, but rather just naïve, self-centered, and ignorant of the cultural significance of what he saw and experienced while in the Powhatan camp. This interpretive approach certainly chimes well with what comes across in Smith's stories. Assuming, then, that something like a "rescue" took place, the question is whether Smith understood what was going on around him, rather than whether it really happened or not. On the specific issue of Pocahontas's role, the editor of Smith's *Complete Works*, Philip L. Barbour, has argued that the rescue episode was likely an initiation ritual taking the form of a mock execution and salvation. In other words, Powhatan may have "adopted" Smith in a ceremony that resembled an execution, perhaps reasoning that one should "keep friends close, but enemies closer." This elegant solution to the "rescue problem," though it does not of itself explain why Smith fails to mention Pocahontas in 1612, has the merit of establishing some continuity between the imprisonment and subsequent friendship between Smith and Powhatan. Citing work on adoption and initiation rituals, Barbour writes that "in Smith's case, Powhatan himself was possibly his foster-father, but Pocahontas had been chosen to act in his stead. . . . Smith could not understand, much less know, this. He simply regarded Pocahontas as his savior."[16]

If the premises are correct, then the conclusion to draw is that Smith's memoirs may be truthful (in the sense that they refer to and relate actual events), while not always being very reliable (in the sense that Smith

does not provide sufficiently informed, impartial, or authoritative interpretations of what he experienced).[17] Thus, the conundrum regarding
the rescue of Smith by Pocahontas can be resolved, at least provisionally,
simply by supposing the blinkered character of Smith's self-centered
interpretations of his adventures: it is entirely possible that such a
"rescue" occurred, but perhaps more likely that it was wholly symbolic;
a rite of passage rather than a planned execution.[18] Of course, this solution
only aggravates the second conundrum: for unless one is prepared to
rest content with the notion that Malick simply lifted his storyline from
the Disney film, one is still left wondering why he tells the story he tells,
in which Smith is not only rescued from certain death, but in which he
and Pocahontas fall in love.[19]

To solve this riddle, we have to return to the relation of the narrative
to the view of nature that Malick presents us with in The New World. For
if nature "itself" manifests itself in the film without covering over its
transformation into history or, conversely, if history is presented as an
expression of nature, then the narrative somehow has to cede ground to
nature in order to compensate for our (natural) tendency to focus on
narrative content rather than "natural content," so to speak. More con-
cretely, Malick's strategy seems to consist in his storyline drawing
attention to the fact that the narrative as such is derivative in relation to
the "real" story of nature that unfolds in the narrative but against its grain.
The triteness and historically inaccurate character of the Disney-like love
story, then—fully accepted by Malick and deliberately woven into his
film—are what indicate to the viewer that the narrative is not an end in
itself and must be put out of play if we are to grasp the true subject of
the film.

Of course, the triteness of a historically implausible love story is
not enough on its own, for we need to be able to distinguish between
"unintentional" and "calculated" triteness. Nor can we depend upon an
infidelity to history to reveal something other than the creative privilege
of the author, in this case Malick, who is in no way obligated to respect
historical fact. But as soon as we look just a little deeper into the film,
Malick's strategy proves to be reinforced by a number of other clues that
he gives us. Not only are there numerous compositional allusions to the
Disney film (such as, the close-up of the compass) and scene repetitions
(such as, the doffing of hats in deference to Pocahontas), but also more
intimate details. In this regard, Malick's decision to cast Irene Bedard as

Pocahontas's mother and Christian Bale as John Rolfe is surely a masterstroke. Both actors were involved in the Disney version of the film: Christian Bale provided the voice of Thomas and Irene Bedard was not only the physical model for Disney's Pocahontas but also provided her voice. In other words, Malick gives us clues that signal to us that his decision to tell the romanticized story was calculated and deliberate.

In other words, within the film and in the articulation of its storyline, the strategic references to Disney's fictionalization of the Pocahontas story are there precisely to discredit the narrative and, more generally, the imaginative stories we tell ourselves in order to justify the particular practices of our communities. Malick seems to be telling us that such legends, reconstructions, "histories," and attempts to make sense of who we are will inevitably prove to be frustratingly vague or exaggerated (like Smith's memoirs) or worse (like the Disney-fication of history) if we overlook the deeper question of the *nature* of human nature that *produces* such stories. Like Nietzsche, we should realize that it is not exactness or truth as such that matter from the standpoint of nature, but just the act of discovering what we call "reason" or "meaning" in chaos; that is, the act of constructing rhythms and forms that help us to live and to survive by creating an understanding of ourselves in our environment. In short, the built-in historical inaccuracies and allusions to the Disney version of the story are meant to lead the viewer from narrative to natural content and thereby to teach us a lesson in human nature: the world of meaning that we invent is only the manifestation of the natural survival mechanism proper to human beings. Strictly speaking, from the standpoint of nature, truth and meaning in history are just nature becoming what it is. Beyond that, nature does not care about our arrows and our guns, our gods, or our wars and revolutions. There are no perspectives "on" nature or stories about human experience that escape the natural character of generating such perspectives and practices.

Or to look at things from a complementary vantage point, it is naturalized reason that is the starting point for truth and meaning—not the particular practices and fallible assumptions of specific self-interpretations and perspectives on nature, be they part of the Old World or the New. The action of the film underscores this by cancelling itself out, by becoming a consciously ironic caricature of an allegedly archetypal story of human experience. To choose the Pocahontas legend as the narrative basis for *The New World*, and to integrate into it the clichéd

Figure 10

love story of Disney's *Pocahontas*, therefore serves to awaken the viewer to the necessary and inescapable process of nature by the ruse of a self-deconstructing narrative: in this way, the narrative itself reveals to us that it communicates this deeper process.

The presentation of this process culminates, at the end of the film, in another fictional scene, set in England shortly before Pocahontas's death in 1617. In a garden on the Rolfe family estate, Pocahontas cavorts with her son, Thomas. She says to herself in her last voiceover: "Mother, now I know where you live." She is answering her own question from the beginning of the film; or rather, the camera answers for her, as the angle changes from the topiary hedges and trees that dominate the last part of the film, stressing the attempted mastery of nature. In an explicit shift of perspective, an orderly hedge gives way to its sinuous branches (Figure 10), and one kind of order yields to another, deeper order, of which it is a part. The image makes clear that human self-understanding—the orderly narratives we construct, the intuition of identity in difference, and even the specificity of cultures and the individuality of people—are all parasitical upon the obscure becoming of nature or what Nietzsche calls the will to power, that is, the *real* "war" in the heart of nature, in which we are no more than pawns, witting or unwitting:

> And do you know what "the world" is to me? Shall I show it to you in my mirror? This world: a monster of energy, without beginning, without end; a firm, iron magnitude of force that does not grow bigger or smaller, that does not expend itself but only transforms

itself; . . . set in a definite space as a definite force, and not a space that might be "empty" here or there, but rather as force throughout, as a play of forces and waves of forces, at the same time one and many, increasing here and at the same time decreasing there; a sea of forces flowing and rushing together, eternally changing, eternally flooding back, with tremendous years of recurrence, with an ebb and a flood of its forms; out of the simplest forms striving toward the most complex . . ., out of the play of contradictions back to the joy of concord. . . .—*This world is the will to power—and nothing besides!* And you yourselves are also this will to power—and nothing besides![20]

Notes

1 See, for example, Orr 1998; McCann 2003; Silberman 2003.

2 Malick translated Heidegger's *Vom Wesen des Grundes* (Heidegger 1969). He studied philosophy under Stanley Cavell at Harvard in the 1960s and intended to write his doctoral thesis on Kierkegaard, Heidegger, and Wittgenstein under Gilbert Ryle at Oxford. Ryle proved unreceptive to the idea. Malick returned to the United States and taught philosophy, and Heidegger specifically, at MIT in the late 1960s, substituting for Hubert Dreyfus. These biographical details are related in Critchley 2005: 98–9. The chapter in question was originally published as Critchley 2002. A slightly revised version of Critchley's paper appears in this collection, pp. 11–27.

3 Critchley 2005: 111 (this volume, p. 26). I am not convinced that our strivings and their mere being are as remote from each other as Critchley suggests, especially in the light of *The New World*.

4 Adorno 1973: 180; Adorno 1997: vol. 6, 181–2. I provide the page number of the English translation of the text for ease of reference, though the quoted text is a retranslation of the original.

5 Nietzsche 1967–1977, 1988: vol. 11, 38 (10): 608. (This edition is hereafter referred to by the abbreviation KSA.)

6 Aristotle 1984: 1332b4–5, vol. 2, 2114.

7 Nietzsche, *KSA*, vol. 11, 41 (11): 687–8.

8 See Nietzsche, *KSA*, vol. 12, 5 (65): 209.

9 It follows from this *not only* that is there no defensible difference within nature between human beings and other animals or plants—according to Nietzsche, there is *not even* a defensible difference between organic nature (plants, animals, humans) and inorganic nature (crystals, galaxies). See Nietzsche, *KSA*, vol. 11, 34 (247): 504.

10 Nietzsche, *KSA*, vol. 11, 34 (247): 503–4.

11 Malick's concept of subjective rationality is left underdetermined in *The New World*. Descartes was born eleven years before Smith met Pocahontas in

Virginia. However, in some ways, Malick's naturalism is a more effective counter to Kantian a priori subjectivity. But these historical points of reference matter little: as we shall see, history is a mere by-product of the human perspective on natural processes. In this context, Malick is implicitly criticizing the *general idea* of a subjective rationality divorced from nature, not the ideas of a particular philosopher.

12 In this way, Malick seems to subscribe to the Nietzschean idea that nature itself blocks us from seeking truth in some realm other than that of sovereign nature: "Nature forbids . . . forced entry [*Eindringen*]." See Nietzsche, *KSA*, vol. 10, 184.

13 Notably Smith's contemporary, David Lloyd, and subsequently Henry Adams, the nineteenth-century American historian, among others.

14 Smith was probably away from the Fort for about twenty-three days in all, only some of which would have been spent in captivity, which Smith variously records as lasting between a month and six weeks. See Barbour's remark on this subject in Smith 1986a, vol. 2, 146, n.2.

15 For an overview of the debate, see Lepore 2007.

16 See Barbour 1969: 24–5. See also Barbour 1964: 167–9; Emerson 1971: 81; Smith, 1986a, vol. 2, 146, n.3. Barbour explains the omission of Pocahontas's name in *The Proceedings* of 1612 by the idea that Smith "still regarded her as a mere child—just one of Powhatan's children." See Barbour 1969: 27.

17 Indeed, Barbour also speaks of Smith's "befuddled recollections, hampered always by his linguistic shortcomings." See Barbour 1969: 25.

18 As Smith was being held as a prisoner, it is also possible that Powhatan contemplated having him killed, but it would be strange to imagine an execution ceremony suddenly and spontaneously transforming into an initiation ceremony.

19 It could be argued that Malick derives his narrative from nineteenth-century antecedents rather than from the Disney film, but since he could not reasonably have assumed audience familiarity with these distortions of the story as they compare with Smith's own accounts, we are still left with the problem of understanding Malick's decision to tell the fictional, romanticized version. Unfortunately, the Disney film, and more generally the romanticized legend, would have been the inevitable point of reference for many viewers.

20 Nietzsche 1968: 549–50; Nietzsche, *KSA*, vol. 11, 38 (12): 610–11. In *The Thin Red Line*, Witt translates these ideas back into their Emersonian form, via a direct quotation from Steinbeck's *The Grapes of Wrath*: "Maybe all men got one big soul ever'body's a part of." Of course, Witt's perspective is not authoritative; it is corrected and complemented by Welsh's more austere materialism: "What difference do you think you can make, one single man in all this madness? If you die, it's gonna be for nothing. There's not some

other world out there where everything's gonna be okay. There's just this
one. Just this rock." Or consider the exchange between Kit and one of the
police officers who arrests him at the end of Badlands: Officer: "You're quite
an individual, Kit." Kit: "Think they'll take that into consideration?"

References

Adorno, T.W. (1973) Negative Dialectics, trans. E.B. Ashton, London: Routledge.
—— (1984) "The idea of natural history," Telos, 60: 111–24.
—— (1997) Gesammelte Schriften, Rolf Tiedemann (ed.), 20 vols, Frankfurt am
Main: Suhrkamp.
Aristotle (1984) Politics, trans. B. Jowett, in Jonathan Barnes (ed.), The Complete
Works of Aristotle, Princeton, NJ: Princeton University Press.
Barbour, P.L. (1964) The Three Worlds of Captain John Smith, Boston, MA: Houghton
Mifflin.
—— (1969) Pocahontas and Her World: a Chronicle of America's First Settlement in which is
Related the Story of the Indians and the Englishmen, Particularly Captain John Smith, Captain
Samuel Argall, and Master John Rolfe, Boston, MA: Houghton Mifflin.
Bersani, L. and U. Dutoit (2004) Forms of Being: Cinema, Aesthetics, Subjectivity, London:
British Film Institute.
Burr, T. (2006) "The New World movie review," Boston Globe, January 20, 2006.
Critchley, S. (2002) "Calm: on Terrence Malick's The Thin Red Line," Film-Philosophy,
6, no. 48.
—— (2005) Things Merely Are, London: Routledge.
Emerson, E.H. (1971) Captain John Smith, New York: Twayne Publishers.
Furstenau, M. and L. MacAvoy (2003) "Terrence Malick's Heideggerian cinema:
war and the question of being in The Thin Red Line," in H. Patterson (ed.) (2003)
The Cinema of Terrence Malick: Poetic Visions of America, London and New York:
Wallflower Press, 173–85.
Heidegger, M. (1969) The Essence of Reasons, trans. T. Malick, bilingual edn,
Evanston, IL: Northwestern University Press.
Hoberman, J. (2006) "Paradise Now," [cited March 31, 2006], available from
http://www.villagevoice.com/film/0610,hoberman,72427,20.html.
Lepore, J. (2007) "Our town," The New Yorker, April 2, 2007, 40–5.
McCann, B. (2003) "'Enjoying the scenery': landscape and the fetishization of
nature in Badlands and Days of Heaven," in H. Patterson (ed.) (2003) The Cinema
of Terrence Malick: Poetic Visions of America, London and New York: Wallflower Press,
75–85.
Nietzsche, F. (1967–77; 1988) Kritische Studienausgabe, G. Colli and M. Montinari
(eds), 2nd edn, 15 vols, Berlin: Walter de Gruyter.
—— (1968) The Will to Power, trans. W. Kaufmann and R.J. Hollingdale, ed.
W. Kaufmann, New York: Vintage Books.
Orr, J. (1998) Contemporary Cinema, Edinburgh: Edinburgh University Press.

Silberman, R. (2003) "Terrence Malick, landscape and 'this war in the heart of nature'," in H. Patterson (ed.) (2003) *The Cinema of Terrence Malick: Poetic Visions of America*, London and New York: Wallflower Press, 160–72.

Smith, J. (1986a) *The Complete Works of Captain John Smith (1580–1631)*, P.L. Barbour (ed.), 3 vols, Chapel Hill, NC: University of North Carolina Press.

—— (1986b) *The Generall historie of Virginia, New-England and the Summer Isles with the names of the Adventurers, Planters, and Governours from their first beginning An: 1584 to this Present 1624*, in P.L. Barbour (ed.) (1986) *The Complete Works of Captain John Smith (1580–1631)*, Chapel Hill, NC: University of North Carolina Press.

—— (1986c) *The Proceedings of the English colonie in Virginia since their first beginning from England in the yeare of our Lord 1606, till this present 1612, with all their accidents that befell them in their Iournies and Discoveries*, in P.L. Barbour (ed.) (1986) *The Complete Works of Captain John Smith (1580–1631)*, Chapel Hill, NC: University of North Carolina Press.

Whalen, T. (1999) "'Maybe all men got one big soul': the hoax within the metaphysics of Terrence Malick's *The Thin Red Line*," *Literature/Film Quarterly*, 27 (3): 162–6.

Zacharek, S. (2006) "The New World" [cited March 31, 2006], available from http://dir.salon.com/story/ent/movies/review/2005/12/23/new_world/index.html.

Index

RELATED TITLES FROM ROUTLEDGE

'Philosophers on Film' series
Talk to Her
Edited by A. W. Eaton

Pedro Almodóvar is one of the most renowned film directors of recent years. *Talk to Her* is one of the most discussed and controversial of all his films. Dealing principally with the issue of rape, it also offers profound insights into the nature of love and friendship whilst raising important philosophical and moral questions in unsettling and often paradoxical ways.

This is the first book to explore and address the philosophical aspects of Almodóvar's film. Opening with a helpful introduction by Noël Carroll that places the film in context, specially commissioned chapters examine the following topics:

- the relationship between art and morality and the problem of 'immoralism'
- moral injury and its role in the way we form moral judgments, including the ethics of love and friendship
- the nature of dialogue, sexual objectification and what 'listening to' means in the context of gender
- Almodóvar's use of allusion and the unmasking of appearances to explore hidden themes in human nature.

Including a biography of Almodóvar, *Talk to Her* is essential reading for students interested in philosophy and film as well as ethics and gender. It is also provides an accessible and informative insight into philosophy for those in related disciplines such as film studies, literature and religion.

Contributors: Noël Carroll, A. W. Eaton, Cynthia Freeland, Robert B. Pippin, C.D.C. Reeve and George M. Wilson

A.W. Eaton is Assistant Professor in Philosophy at the University of Illinois at Chicago. She has published articles on the relationship between ethics and aesthetics, pornography and feminist aesthetics.

ISBN 10: 0-415-77366-0 (hbk)
ISBN 10: 0-415-77367-9 (pbk)

ISBN 13: 978-0-415-77366-9 (hbk)
ISBN 13: 978-0-415-77367-6 (pbk)

Available at all good bookshops
For ordering and further information please visit:
www.routledge.com

Thinking on Screen
Film as Philosophy
Thomas E. Wartenberg

'This book is a powerful defense of the view that films can philosophize. Characterized by its clear and lively presentation, and by its intertwining of philosophical argument with detailed discussion of several important films, it will be of interest not just to those studying philosophy and film but to everyone who believes in the importance of film to our cognitive life.'

Berys Gaut, *University of St Andrews*

Thinking on Screen: Film as Philosophy is an accessible and thought-provoking examination of the way films raise and explore complex philosophical ideas.

Beginning with a demonstration of how specific forms of philosophical discourse are presented cinematically, Wartenberg moves on to offer a systematic account of the ways in which specific films undertake the task of philosophy. Focusing on the films *The Man Who Shot Liberty Valance, Modern Times, The Matrix, Eternal Sunshine of the Spotless Mind, The Third Man, The Flicker* and *Empire*, Wartenberg shows how these films express meaningful and pertinent philosophical ideas.

Thinking on Screen: Film as Philosophy is essential reading for students of philosophy with an interest in film, aesthetics and film theory. It will also be of interest to film enthusiasts intrigued by the philosophical implications of film.

Thomas E. Wartenberg is Professor at Mount Holyoke College and author of *Unlikely Couples: Movie Romance as Social Criticism* and *The Forms of Power*.

ISBN 10: 0–4157730–6 (hbk)
ISBN 10: 0–41577431–4 (pbk)
ISBN 10: 0–20303062–1 (ebk)

ISBN 13: 978–0–415–77430–7 (hbk)
ISBN 13: 978–0–415–77431–4 (pbk)
ISBN 13: 978–0–203–03062–2 (ebk)

Available at all good bookshops
For ordering and further information please visit:
www.routledge.com